Intelligence Mastery

The Ultimate 21-Day Guide to Increase your EQ, Improve your Social Skills and Communication at Work and Master Your Emotions

Judith Yandell

Copyright © 2019 Judith Yandell

All rights reserved.

In no way is it legal to reproduce, duplicate, or transmit any part of this document in either electronic means or in printed format. recording of this publication is strictly prohibited and any storage of this document is not allowed unless with written permission from the publisher. all rights reserved. The information provided herein is stated to be truthful and consistent, in that any liability, in terms of inattention or otherwise, by any usage or abuse of any policies, processes, or directions contained within is the solitary and utter responsibility of the recipient reader. under no circumstances will any legal responsibility or blame be held against the publisher for any reparation, damages, or monetary loss due to the information herein, either directly or indirectly. Respective authors own all copyrights not held by the publisher. The information herein is offered for informational purposes solely, and is universal as so. the presentation of the information is without contract or any type of guarantee assurance. The trademarks that are used are without any consent, and the publication of the trademark is without permission or backing by the trademark owner. all trademarks and brands within this book are for clarifying purposes only and are the owned by the owners themselves, not affiliated with this document.

TABLE OF CONTENTS

Introduction 7
Day 1: Mastering Emotional Awareness 13
Day 2: How to Develop Emotional Assessment 19
Day 3: Gauging Your Emotional Needs 23
Day 4: Learning to Manage Your Emotional States 29
Day 5: How To Develop Self-Confidence 35
Day 6: Everything About Optimism 39
Day 7: Mastering Self-Control 43
Day 8: Why Conscientiousness Matters 47
Day 9: Increase Your Social Awareness 51
Day 10: How to Develop Your Empathy 55
Day 11: The Keys of Effective Communication 59
Day 12: Forming Positive and Meaningful Bonds With Other People 63
Day 13: How To Build and Maintain Trust 67
Day 14: Working Together To Accomplish a Common Goal . 71
Day 15: Resolving Conflicts 75
Day 16: How to Become Adaptable 79
Day 17: What is Innovativeness 83
and How to Master it 83
Day 18: Initiate Change in Your Environment 87
Day 19: How to Find Your Source of Motivation and Inspiration 91
Day 20: Don't Stop Improving Yourself 97
Day 21: Learning to Accept Situations That Are Out of Your Control 101
Conclusion 105
Other Books by Judith Yandell 108

Introduction

I would like to thank you for purchasing this copy of *Emotional Intelligence Mastery: The Ultimate 21-Day Guide to Increase your EQ, Improve your Social Skills and Communication at Work, and Master Your Emotions*. I would also like to offer you a short congratulations for taking the first steps on the way to mastering emotional intelligence and living a more emotionally satisfying and fulfilling life. *The Ultimate 21-Day Guide to Increase your EQ, Improve your Social Skills and Communication at Work, and Master Your Emotions* will be your guide in this journey and will give you all of the tools you need to do exactly what it says on the cover.

Naturally, this book will help you to find the tools necessary in order to master your social skills and communication at work, as well as your emotions, which will in turn increase what is known as your "E.Q.", or "Emotional Quotient. A person's emotional quotient is an objective measure of the level of their emotional intelligence. It is typically represented as a score from a standardized examination of, of course, their emotional intelligence. Although, and arguably more important than simply having and maintaining a high EQ score, attaining high levels of emotional intelligence and emotional control can benefit your own life and those of the people around you in many ways, that you might not even think of as connected to emotional states. Obviously, having a good knowledge of the emotional triggers that you and the people around you possess can help you to understand which things or situations you actually enjoy, as well as the ones that you might not particularly enjoy, or even ones that you might want to avoid altogether. At an even deeper level, you may even eventually become capable of handling more difficult or stressful sorts of situations more effectively, and without becoming panicked or even overwhelmed. Many individuals may also tend to lean toward the opposite end of the spectrum, and will then start to ignore or repress their own emotions and avoid honest reactions altogether, so as to "protect" them from any possible negative reactions or results of said reactions. This is, of course, completely counterproductive, and is itself a bad habit. It could also, paradoxically, be considered a negative result of emotional repression on its own, and may even lead to even worse or extreme reactions and negative effects on one's life later on. Repressing these sorts of emotional signals can even lead to a whole host of negative effects such as;

- Unnecessary or excessive stress
- Increased blood pressure
- Anxiety
- Depression
- Alcohol and/or drug addictions
- And possibly more similar or even worse symptoms.

On the other hand, though, gaining a high level of emotional intelligence can not only help to fight off those types of issues but can actively benefit you in many ways. A good EQ or a high level of emotional intelligence can manifest in the forms of decreased stress levels, fewer problems occurring in your day-to-day life, better self-control and self-esteem, a better social life and improved social interactions, and simply as just a better mood and having more energy throughout the day to get things done and enjoy your life. You may even see more opportunities come your way!

With all of that said, though, it may even be possible that you are already more emotionally intelligent than you realize, even if you are currently suffering from one or more of the negative symptoms referred to above, or another example of a negative reaction of these sorts. There are, however, ways to deal with these kinds of problems. Naturally, the first step to solving these issues is to recognize and understand them, so you will know what you actually need to do about them. Understanding your emotions can be confusing and somewhat difficult, especially for those who are not used to paying attention to that sort of thing. However, once you know what to look out for, it becomes much easier to pick up on the signs or clues, and your reactions to various internal and external triggers.

The next step, once you have learned to recognize your emotional states, is to gain a proper understanding of where they come from and what triggers might lead to which reactions from you, and even others. This understanding will give you access to the tools that you need to actually take care of yourself and deal with these reactions, whether it be in removing yourself from a particular situation or even solving a problem that you did not even realize was actually important to you. Once you have learned to understand and solve problems as they arise, you can even anticipate the needs of yourself and the people around you so as to avoid any problems that may arise in the future, and assure that you have the tools necessary for allowing yourself to live the most emotionally satisfying and fulfilling life that you can.

Additionally, this book will go over some other skills that can be useful in your daily life as well. It will cover valuable skills relating to your own personal emotional intelligence, such as:

- Self-Control and managing your emotional states,
- The concept of optimism and the law of attraction,
- Self-confidence and being more comfortable in unfamiliar situations,
- Conscientiousness and owning your mistakes and achievements alike,

Social skills to help you communicate more effectively, such as;

- Social awareness and empathy,
- Effective communication methods,
- Forming valuable bonds and building trust,
- Working with others, and resolving or preventing conflicts,

And even concepts like

- Adaptability,
- Innovativeness,
- Finding and maintaining motivation and staying driven
- Pushing yourself and striving for excellence
- And Accepting situations and things that are out of your control.

The Ultimate 21-Day Guide to Increase your EQ, Improve your Social Skills and Communication at Work, and Master Your Emotions is, as it says on the cover, a guide to improving your emotional intelligence and social skills, which will cover 21 separate and extremely valuable lessons on this subject over the course of the aforementioned 21 days. As such, each lesson will be covered in its own day, so as to give you time to learn and master these skills.

The first four days will cover their own part of a larger lesson on how to properly handle any situation that may arise and will be useful in all following lessons over the whole of the 21 days and lessons covered in the book. They will each cover their own section of how to handle issues that may arise, in the form of

- Recognizing
- Analyzing
- Understanding, and
- Acting

These lessons will likely be carried over into subsequent days, and every one of the lessons that come after will also be applicable on any given day, as situations may arise that require you to use skills learned previously. The goal of this book is to foster personal growth, and each lesson may even be revisited after the book has been finished if you find it necessary. With that said, though, please continue reading, and if you enjoy the rest of the book, make sure to leave a short review on Amazon. I would love to hear your thoughts!

Day 1:
Mastering Emotional Awareness

The first step to take in order to raise your emotional intelligence, and in turn, your emotional quotient, is to achieve a mastery of emotional awareness. Emotional awareness is, put simply, the ability to recognize your current emotional state, as well as the emotional states of other individuals, and how it changes in response to certain external stimuli. This may seem like a fairly simple and straightforward task, but sometimes it is not as easy to accomplish as one might think.

Emotional awareness is the ability to actively recognize and make sense of not only your emotional states and the way they change but also those of other people around you. This awareness is a large component of what is referred to as 'emotional intelligence,' which also includes the knowledge of how to solve problems in life by understanding emotions. This includes being able to regulate your own emotions and help others out when they may be feeling low, as well. Naturally you will not be able to find effective solutions to these sorts of complicated issues, and subsequently know what action needs to be taken in order to rectify them properly if you do not even understand what the actual problem is, or its root cause. In a lot of cases, there may even be multiple root causes underneath a given problem as it appears on the surface, especially if the issue at hand happens to be a particularly complicated or difficult one.

Gaining a proper mastery over your own emotional awareness can allow you the ability to learn more from your feelings and emotions, as well as their results and causes, much more effectively. For example, if you happen to be, seemingly inexplicably, feeling some form of sadness or possibly even irritation or anger, you can reflect on why this is and make good, informed decisions, based on that information. These decisions might even then be able to help you to understand your emotional states, and how to handle them when they may come up in the future. Good awareness and understanding of the emotional states and triggers possessed by yourself and others around you can even help you in learning to predict your own emotions, as well as those of other individuals, in advance. If you know what situations might lead to a specific emotional response or reaction, you can then learn to be able to plan for them in advance with the knowledge of how to make the best choices possible for the sake of the emotional wellness of yourself and the people around you.

Many people prefer to ignore their emotions completely, choosing to view any sort of acknowledgment of their existence at all as a sign of weakness. This is, however, extremely counterproductive. This sort of emotional self-neglect, and even choosing to remain ignorant of other people's emotional states, can be detrimental to your personal growth, as well as theirs. Not only can it be detrimental to personal growth, becoming aware of the emotional states of yourself and other individuals can show many varied and unexpected benefits in almost all aspects of life. It may even be arguable that emotional awareness is the default, and refusing to gain this awareness and choosing to ignore and neglect it can be actively detrimental for many reasons. I'm sure you have, at some point, heard the saying, "Humans are social animals by nature." This is absolutely a truthful statement. We come into the world as a result of the actions of other individuals and are then dependent on those people, as well. We spend a large portion of our lives being taught by and teaching other people, and even more, time is spent communicating with other people. Whether we like it or not, there are very few moments in our lives, if any, during which we are not affected by the actions and choices of other people. For these reasons, it is not very surprising at all that a large portion of our happiness as people comes from, in the company of, and the context of our relationships with others. We spend large portions of our lives searching for relationships and love, or forming friendships and bonds, or even simply working, all alongside and in the company of those around us. For these reasons, among others even, neglecting one's emotional states is actively doing themselves a disservice as well as everyone around them. Everything you do affects everyone you interact with in some way or another. Additionally, for creatures who seem to spend a very large majority of their lives interacting with others, being clued in about the emotional states of yourself and others, and possessing good social skills can be vital for maintaining a positive lifestyle and leading a healthy, happy life.

Naturally, then, these sorts of emotional skills will be very important tools for improving your emotional intelligence, no matter what level you may be at the present moment. As such, the first few days will be dedicated to giving you the tools necessary in order to do this. This initial lesson will be split up into four days, with each day covering one part of it. The first day is going to cover what is referred to as "emotional awareness."

There are five commonly accepted levels of emotional awareness. The first is in being aware of physical sensations as a reaction to external stimuli. What this means is that you are aware of the physical sensations tied to certain emotions. This can take the form of a change in your heartbeat or temperature, or feeling nauseated, sick, or even feeling "butterflies" in your stomach. At this stage, a common reaction may be something similar to thinking, "My stomach feels sick for some reason. I do not understand why."

The second level is being aware of your "action tendencies." Obviously, this includes the tendencies of other people as well. What this means, though, is that at this level of emotional awareness, you will be aware of what reactions you may have to certain events or situations. You know what you like and do not like, and which situations you prefer to avoid, or ones that you enjoy. At this level, you might find yourself in an uncomfortable situation and think, "I do not like being here right now. This is unpleasant. I would like to go home and be comfortable."

The third tier (as well as the fourth and fifth) is a little bit deeper than the first and second levels of emotional awareness. Level three is about actually being aware of emotions. At this stage, you are aware of singular primary emotions that you may be feeling at a given moment. This includes emotions like happy, sad, and angry. A good example of this level of emotional understanding might sound something like being in a pleasant place and thinking, "I like it here. The environment makes me feel happy."

The fourth stage, naturally, is one step further and involves understanding multiple emotions and various intensities of emotions, as well. You may understand multiple kinds of emotions from multiple sources, and the contrasting feelings that may come along with them, but may not be capable of complete understanding of what they mean or how another individual may feel about the same scenario. This level of emotional awareness might sound something like, "I'm not having fun here, but my friend seems to be enjoying it enough, and I suppose I'm glad for that."

At the fifth and last stage of emotional awareness, you are able to discern multiple levels and layers of emotions from a number of sources and accurately describe them to others if needed. You may use metaphors or other ways of relating these concepts to other people in ways that they will understand, and you can completely relate to the emotional states of other people around you, and their sources as well as the intricacies of how to manage them and help others to understand and manage as well.

Naturally, this sort of comprehension may take time to grasp completely. As such, today's task will be carried out over the course of multiple days, as it is an extremely vital component of gaining a proper understanding of emotional states and improving your Emotional Intelligence and, subsequently, your EQ. The actual task for today (and the days following) will be simply to keep these levels of emotional awareness in mind as you go throughout your day and gauge where you stand on the scale mentioned above, as well as why you fall where you do. Each level of emotional awareness has its own specific goals and tasks to work on and will be carried out over up to five days, taking one day for each level beyond the one that you happen to be at on the first day. The tasks to be carried out over the next few days can be accomplished alongside today's goals as well, and are designed to be finished in this manner.

If you are at the first level, you should be looking out for the physical reactions that you may have in response to specific triggers. Consider why this is, and which emotions they are tied to. If you feel sick to your stomach, you should be trying to understand why you feel that way and consider your typical reaction is to this sensation.

If you fall under the second tier, the task will be to look out for your "action tendencies," and evaluate why you would want to leave an uncomfortable situation, and understand the emotional root is that this reaction is connected to.

For the third level of emotional awareness, the goal is to recognize emotional states as they occur from inciting external stimuli. Consider how you feel and react to specific events as they happen, and what sort of state they promote in yourself, emotionally. Try to understand how conflicting events might make you feel, and the various ranges of emotional reactions you may experience, both in nature as well as intensity.

For the fourth stage, you should be looking for situations throughout the day that elicit strong reactions, not only from yourself but also from others around you. Try to gauge how they might feel in these scenarios and how they might react or feel in response. You should be attempting to go through the previous days again, while also considering the emotional states and reactions of other individuals.

Once you have reached the fifth, and last level of emotional awareness, you have got it down and can exhibit a competent understanding of all of the skills talked about in this chapter. You should still be taking these skills into consideration during daily life, however, as they are not ones that can always be mastered in just a few days. Practice does make perfect, after all, and you should always be striving to better yourself in any and every way that you can.

Day 2:
How To Develop Emotional Assessment

Today will cover a concept that is very similar and connected to what you learned about in yesterday's chapter. The assignment will be covering the topic of emotional assessment, rather than simply awareness. The best way to think about and understand the idea of emotional assessment is as an extension of emotional awareness, rather than its own separate concept. Naturally, the next step after acknowledging and becoming aware of your emotional states (as well as the emotional states of those around you) would be to consider then and gain a proper understanding of those emotions.

Emotional assessment is the second section of the four-part lesson designed to give you the tools necessary to ensure that you can possess the ability to handle any situation, no matter how stressful or uncomfortable, and ultimately grow as a person and maximize your potential for emotional intelligence as well as your EQ. Emotional assessment can be defined as the evaluation of nature, origin, and meaning behind the emotional states of oneself as well as others around them. What this means is that once you have begun to gain an awareness of your emotional states, you can learn to question their origins and meanings. This skill will be very important down the road, as simply acknowledging and recognizing your emotions will not allow you to do very much unless you also have the ability to know where these sorts of emotions come from, what they mean on a deeper level, and what to do about them as they arise. Additionally, emotional awareness can be a valuable tool for pushing your emotional intelligence (as well as your emotional quotient) even further. Future goals to be completed over the following days will also rely on a solid understanding and mastery over this skill and the ones that are associated with it.

Today's lesson of "emotional assessment" will be carried out alongside the assignment from the first day. As such, this assignment for today will also very likely need to be completed over multiple days. You will need to begin working on this skill starting on the second day (as this is, in fact, the assignment for the second day of *The Ultimate 21-Day Guide to Increase your EQ, Improve your Social Skills and Communication at Work, and Master Your Emotions*) of the assignment from the first day. Additionally, the first day's assignment only goes through one day for each level of emotional awareness, beginning with the second day. This is because the first tier is the lowest, and each day's individual assignment focuses on improving the corresponding stage of emotional awareness and beginning to understand the next tier up on the ladder of emotional awareness. Today's assignment, however, will need to begin on the second day of the assignment that was to begin on the first day and continue through the day after the last day of the first assignment. For example, if you begin the lesson from day one at the first level of emotional awareness, you will end up doing four days of this assignment, with it having a structure that looks something like;

- Day 1: Levels one and two
- Day 2: Levels two and three
- Day 3: Levels three and four
- Day 4: levels four and five

Whereas today's assignment, as mentioned previously, will need to continue for an extra day and begin a day later, and will end up being closer to the list shown below:

- Day 1: Levels one and two
- Day 2: Levels two and three, assessment for level two
- Day 3: Levels three and four, assessment for level three
- Day 4: Levels four and five, assessment for level four
- Day 5: All five levels, assessment for level five and all previous levels.

As far as the actual assignment for today (and the next few days, as is required according to the list above) goes, you will need to spend time throughout the day, or days, working on your emotional awareness. As you make progress with these skills, you should also be making an effort to consider why you react in the ways that you do, and why which of your emotional responses occur as a result to which external triggers. What are the root causes behind these emotional reactions, and what do they mean. Why do some specific external triggers elicit stronger or milder responses from you or other people around you? How would other people around you feel about or even react to a specific situation? You should be asking questions similar to these ones that relate to the current day's tasks and lessons. The important thing is to be asking why, in regards to your emotional states and reactions, and considering them in terms of their origins and how to handle them now as well as in the future. This task will, as previously stated, need to be completed for each level of the skills learned in the chapter on emotional awareness.

Day 3:
Gauging Your Emotional Needs

The assignment from yesterday was all about using your newfound skill of emotional awareness to begin to understand and assess your emotional states, as well as their meanings and origins. Today's lesson will be taking that idea and pushing it another step further. Today's chapter will be about gauging your emotional needs. Naturally, it will also be applicable for other people and will give you the tools necessary to gauge the emotional needs of any person or individual you may need to do so for.

Gauging your emotional needs will entail using your knowledge of emotional awareness, starting from the third stage of emotional awareness, as well as the newly learned skill of emotional assessment, in order to begin to understand what it is that you need or would like to do based on your emotional states. You will need to pay particularly close attention to the "action tendencies" from the second stage of emotional awareness, which this book talked about in the first chapter. What it actually means to gauge the emotional means of yourself and other people around you is to use the knowledge of your action tendencies and emotional awareness as a whole, as well as the things you might learn during an assessment of your emotional states and their meanings, to actually understand them and what they signify for you or, naturally, whichever individual may be experiencing these emotions in a particular moment. Additionally, a good mastery of this skill will allow you to know what you might actually need to do, or how you may want to proceed moving forward when you experience these types of emotions or emotional reactions in response to external stimuli in the future. This is useful, of course, because as the third section of the four-part lesson on how to gain the tools to deal with difficult or uncomfortable situations and raise your level of emotional intelligence, it will help you to understand how to solve any problems that you may encounter. It will also be a vital step on the way to this goal, as you can't take effective action to solve these sorts of problems and rectify difficult or problematic situations unless you have a complete and proper understanding of what the problem is and how to actually fix or handle it once you do gain this sort of understanding.

This assignment is another one that will be carried out along with the first two, starting on the third day. It will also need to continue for an extra day, as with the assignment from the second chapter. This can become somewhat confusing, of course, as the schedule for these tasks is dependent on the stage you began at on the first day and can change a bit depending on where you may be at. This assignment should always be started on the third day of *The Ultimate 21-Day Guide to Increase your EQ, Improve your Social Skills and Communication at Work, and Master Your Emotions*, as it is the third chapter and designed to be for the third day of this 21-day journey on the way toward mastering your emotional intelligence and raising your emotional quotient. As was stated previously, this assignment may begin to get somewhat confusing, due to the schedule of the multiple-day assignment from the first chapter and day. As such, there will be a short guide below on how to proceed with this task, which will be dependent on the schedule from the past two days' assignments.

Today's assignment will be to use the skill of emotional assessment from the lesson on day two to take your emotional intelligence another step further. On the third day, you will begin to gauge your emotional needs. What this will entail is using the knowledge you gained previously to consider what you may need, moving forward. Think about what you tend to do in these types of uncomfortable or unfamiliar situations, and whether that is a healthy reaction or not. Additionally, you will need to consider what the best action would be to take on a long-term basis, as well as for the sake of your emotional well-being in the present moment. The goal for this assignment is to simply practice being cognizant of your emotional states and what they mean for you, as well as how you should proceed when you experience these emotions in the future.

If you began *The Ultimate 21-Day Guide to Increase your EQ, Improve your Social Skills and Communication at Work, and Master Your Emotions* on the first level of emotional awareness, then the schedule for the assignment from the second day will look like the one below;

- Day 1: Levels one and two
- Day 2: Levels two and three, assessment for level two
- Day 3: Levels three and four, assessment for level three
- Day 4: Levels four and five, assessment for level four
- Day 5: All five levels, assessment for level five and all previous levels.

With this schedule listed above, the assignment from today's chapter, which will continue for an additional day, will look more like this:

- Day 1: Levels one and two
- Day 2: Levels two and three, assessment for level two
- Day 3: Levels three and four, assessment for level three, Gauging emotional needs
- Day 4: Levels four and five, assessment for level four, gauging emotional needs
- Day 5: All five levels, assessment for level five and all previous levels, gauging emotional needs.

However, if you began the first day with the second level of emotional awareness, for example, the schedule changes a little bit, and will look more like this:

- Day 1: Levels two and three
- Day 2: Levels three and four, assessment for level three
- Day 3: Levels four and five, assessment for level four, gauging emotional needs
- Day 4: All levels up to the fifth, assessment for level five and all previous levels, gauging emotional needs

Or, taking it another step (or three steps, depending on which level of emotional awareness you started day one's assignment on) further, if you began the first day's assignment with the third, fourth, or fifth level of emotional awareness, your schedule for these goals or tasks will change even more. In that case, your schedule for today's task will look closer to this one, shown below:

- Day 1: Levels three and four, levels four and five, or all levels up to level five, if begun at level five

- Day 2: Levels four and five or all levels up to the fifth, assessment for level four or level five and all previous levels
- Day 3: All levels up to the fifth, assessment for level five and all previous levels, Gauging emotional needs

The multiple-day schedule for the assignment from the first chapter, as you can see, will change based on which day you started on. However, at this stage, it will always need to take at least three days. When tomorrow's goal is covered, it will also add another day, changing the number of days to complete from three to four. Unless, of course, you began at the first stage of emotional awareness, in which case it will take five days to complete, with the fifth day bleeding into the next section on the fifth chapter. This will, however, only take an extra day at most, and chapter five's assignment will be a fairly straightforward one as well. With that said, practice does make perfect, as said before, and these tasks can be revisited on any future day as needed.

Day 4:
Learning To Manage Your Emotional States

The assignment from yesterday was all about using your newfound skill to gauge the emotional needs of yourself and others to begin to understand, assess, and discern the source and meaning of your emotional states, as well as how you should handle them when they arise. Today's lesson will be the last part of the first section of *The Ultimate 21-Day Guide to Increase your EQ, Improve your Social Skills and Communication at Work, and Master Your Emotions*, which is designed to give you the skills and tools necessary to completely understand and master the goals to be set in the following 17 chapters. This lesson will be taking those ideas and pushing them yet another step further. Today's chapter will be about actually taking action and learning to manage your emotional states. Naturally, it will also be applicable to other people as well and will give you the tools necessary to manage your emotions and emotional states as needed.

Managing your emotional states will entail using your knowledge of emotional awareness, starting from the third stage of emotional awareness, and emotional assessment as well as your newly learned skill of gauging your emotional needs in order to begin to take action and gain control of the emotions of yourself and help the people around you to do the same thing and help themselves as well. Again, you will need to pay close attention to the "action tendencies," referred to in the second level of emotional awareness talked about in the first chapter of this book. What it actually means to manage the emotions and emotional states of yourself and the people around you is to use the knowledge of the action tendencies mentioned earlier, your emotional awareness as a whole, the skills you learned during the assessment of your emotional states and their meanings, and the conclusions or solutions you reached while gauging your emotional needs to understand how to take action effectively, and of course, actually take action to take control of your emotions and help yourself in improving your social skills and communication, mastering your emotions and increasing your emotional intelligence and your emotional quotient.

This assignment is another one that will need to be carried out along with the first three, starting on the fourth day. It will also need to continue for an extra day, as with the assignment from the second and third chapters. This can become somewhat confusing, of course, as the schedule for these tasks is dependent on the stage you began at on the first day and can change a little bit depending on where you may be at. This assignment should always be started on the fourth day of *The Ultimate 21-Day Guide to Increase your EQ, Improve your Social Skills and Communication at Work, and Master Your Emotions*, as it is the fourth chapter of this book and, as such, is designed to be for the fourth day of this 21-day journey on the way toward mastering your emotional intelligence and raising your emotional quotient. As was stated previously, this assignment may begin to get somewhat confusing, due to the schedule of the multiple-day assignment from the first chapter on the day. As such, there will be a short guide below on how to proceed with this task, which will be dependent on the schedule from the past two days' assignments.

Today's assignment will be to use the skills of emotional assessment and gauging needs from the lesson on day two to take your emotional intelligence another step further. On the fourth day, you will begin to gauge your emotional needs and use that information to take action in managing those emotions. You should be actively choosing to remove yourself from uncomfortable situations or try to be putting yourself on ones that help your emotional states when you decide on a certain solution or action to take in response to your emotional assessments and the conclusions that come from them. The goal for this assignment is to simply practice being active about improving your emotional states and promoting positivity for the sake of yourself and the people around you.

If you began *The Ultimate 21-Day Guide to Increase your EQ, Improve your Social Skills and Communication at Work, and Master Your Emotions* on the first level of emotional awareness, then the schedule for the assignment from the second and third days will look like the one below;

- Day 1: Levels one and two
- Day 2: Levels two and three, assessment for level two
- Day 3: Levels three and four, assessment for level three, Gauging emotional needs
- Day 4: Levels four and five, assessment for level four, gauging emotional needs,
- Day 5: All five levels, assessment for level five and all previous levels, gauging emotional needs

With this schedule listed above, the assignment from today's chapter, which will continue on for an additional day, will look more like this:

- Day 1: Levels one and two
- Day 2: Levels two and three, assessment for level two

- Day 3: Levels three and four, assessment for level three, Gauging emotional needs
- Day 4: Levels four and five, assessment for level four, gauging emotional needs, managing emotions
- Day 5: All five levels, assessment for level five and all previous levels, gauging emotional needs, managing emotions

However, if you began the first day with the second level of emotional awareness, for example, the schedule changes a little bit, and will look more like this:

- Day 1: Levels two and three
- Day 2: Levels three and four, assessment for level three
- Day 3: Levels four and five, assessment for level four, gauging emotional needs
- Day 4: All levels up to the fifth, assessment for level five and all previous levels, gauging emotional needs, managing emotions

Or, taking it another step (or three steps, depending on which level of emotional awareness you started day one's assignment on) further, if you began the first day's assignment with the third, fourth, or fifth level of emotional awareness, your schedule for these goals or tasks will change even more. In that case, your schedule for today's task will look closer to this one, shown below:

- Day 1: Levels three and four, levels four and five, or all levels up to level five, if begun at level five
- Day 2: Levels four and five or all levels up to the fifth, assessment for level four or level five and all previous levels
- Day 3: All levels up to the fifth, assessment for level five and all previous levels, Gauging emotional needs

- Day 4: All levels up to the fifth, assessment for level five and all previous levels, gauging emotional needs, managing emotions.

The multiple-day schedule for the assignment from the first chapter, as you can see, will change based on which day you started on. However, at this stage, it will always need to take at least four days. The assignment from today added to the schedule from yesterday and the past few days. It will also add another day, changing the minimum number of days to complete from three to four. Unless, of course, you began at the first stage of emotional awareness, in which case it will take five days to complete, with the fifth day bleeding into the next section on the fifth chapter. This will, however, only take an extra day at most, and chapter five's assignment will be a fairly straightforward one as well. With that said, practice does make perfect, as said before, and these tasks can be revisited on any future day as needed.

Day 5:
How To Develop Self-Confidence

Congratulations! You have finished the first section of *The Ultimate 21-Day Guide to Increase your EQ, Improve your Social Skills and Communication at Work, and Master Your Emotions*! You now have all of the tools necessary to understand and accomplish each of the 17 remaining days' tasks and goals, and are well on your way to completing this journey of personal growth and self-improvement. Additionally, this is the last possible day that you will need to spend completing the five-day schedule created for chapter one's topic of emotional awareness, assuming you began the first chapter with only the first level of emotional awareness.

With all of that said and out of the way, however, today's chapter will be covering the topic of self-confidence. Self-confidence can be defined as a feeling of trust in one's abilities, qualities, and judgment. In this case, the term "self-confidence" will be used in the context of emotional intelligence and in relation to the emotional intelligence and the knowledge and mastery of emotional awareness, assessment, understanding, and management. This is an extremely important part of mastering your emotions and raising your emotional intelligence and your emotional quotient, as it may be difficult to accomplish some or even all of the goals to be set on future days' assignments if you are not sure of yourself, as well as your abilities and perception, and judgment. How can you be expected to take this type of action in order to better yourself in the ways that are aimed for in *The Ultimate 21-Day Guide to Increase your EQ, Improve your Social Skills and Communication at Work, and Master Your Emotions*, if you are not literally confident enough to do the work involved in the first place, after all?

Of course, it can be somewhat annoying to hear "just be confident," sometimes. It does get said with an almost irritating frequency, and in situations that sometimes may not seem to call for it. However, and of course, this one is another of those annoying sayings, it is a cliché for a reason! Confidence really is key with these kinds of self-growth- and personal improvement- based goals. The goal is not even necessarily to become some sort of narcissist or develop a giant, over-the-top ego. It is simply to unburden yourself with any of the troubles involved with the lack of confidence in oneself. True confidence in one's abilities and self should feel, to emotional health, more like what not having a cold is to be physically healthy. In this scenario, self-confidence is simply the default, and being burdened by insecurity is likened to physical illness. Being self-confident, much like the blessing of not actively being burdened by the symptoms of a cold or flu, should not actually be noticed by the individual who experiences them. After all, you do not very often find yourself paying active attention to the lack of physical illness of this sort, do you? However, with all of that said, it is acceptable, and even encouraged to experience some form of pride, satisfaction, or simply relief when one begins to improve in these valuable qualities and skills.

That is actually what this chapter will be all about, too. A large component, and arguably even the key to mastering self-confidence, is positivity. Maintaining a positive attitude, even in situations that may seem somewhat bleak, will allow you to continue to stay motivated and determined to continue pushing yourself and find effective solutions to these sorts of situations. As such, and keeping all of this in mind, the assignment for today will be to attempt to be more positive throughout the day and improve your self-confidence along the way. There are a number of methods of improving one's self-confidence, including some methods that you may not expect to be very helpful at all, and even ones that some individuals actively dismiss as false. These methods include doing things such as;

Standing or sitting upright. There have been many studies showing that simply standing or sitting with a proper, upright posture can improve your moods, self-confidence, and even awareness. When you hold yourself high like this, it can send signals throughout your body and brain that there is some form of external stimuli in the immediate environment that you need to pay attention to. It can cause you to be more aware and alert, more "tuned in" to conversations you may be having, and even simply boost your mood. It can, in doing the act of holding a good posture alone, improve your moods and confidence in yourself. Not to mention, it is much better for your back as well.

Exercise regularly. Now, I know how this one can be perceived. It seems like everyone is always telling their friends to exercise, or go to the gym, or making plans only to have them fall apart a week later. However, if you can go out and get exercise for your own sake, and for the sake of your happiness, as well as your physical and even emotional well-being, it will definitely help. If you do it right, going for a jog once a day, or taking a little walk and just getting out of the house can boost your mood and your confidence in yourself so much more than you might realize! People need that sort of release, and it can be a great way to unwind and even meditate, in a sense. There is something almost calming about going for a nice walk, jog, or swim. Activities like that almost always instill a sense of tranquility, and possibly even satisfaction, and that's really what this chapter is about. Arguably, even, this book as a whole.

Give yourself permission to take risks and make mistakes. Many people tend to think about themselves in the context of and compare themselves to other people. Often, these comparisons will favor the other person or people by a wide margin. We might think that the people around you are so much more happy, creative, successful, etc. than yourself. What we do not tend to consider is that failure is an inherent part of accomplishing our goals, and it takes time to do the sorts of things involved in improving your emotional states and emotional intelligence. Even people who might excel in certain areas are very likely to be struggling with others. Nobody is perfect, and we can't be good at everything. It is important to give yourself time to improve, and not to be afraid to make mistakes.

There are many more things you can do to improve your self-confidence, but the important thing is simply to give yourself time. Obviously, one or all of these examples may be carried on after today. In the case of the second example, exercise, that one will need to continue on after today. There really is not a way to do that one in a single day without overexerting yourself. The thing to keep in mind during today is that you should be keeping in mind ways to improve your self-confidence that you can accomplish in your daily life. As you encounter difficulties or trying situations throughout the day, consider how you can help yourself in this way and ways like it. Try holding a good posture at work, or go for a run in the morning. You should be doing whatever it is you may need to in order to help yourself. It is all about you, and your own personal happiness, growth, and well-being.

Day 6:
Everything About Optimism

During yesterday's chapter of *Ultimate 21-Day Guide to Increase your EQ, Improve your Social Skills and Communication at Work, and Master Your Emotions*, the topic of self-confidence was discussed. This is a valuable skill, as a feeling of trust in one's abilities, qualities, and judgment can be extremely helpful in mastering your emotions and raising your emotional intelligence and your emotional quotient. It may be difficult to accomplish some or even all of the goals to be set on today and the next 15 days' assignments if you are not sure of yourself, as well as your abilities, perception, and judgment. How can you be expected to take this type of action in order to better yourself in the ways that are aimed for in *The Ultimate 21-Day Guide to Increase your EQ, Improve your Social Skills and Communication at Work, and Master Your Emotions*, if you are not literally confident enough to do the work involved in the first place, after all?

However, today's chapter of *Ultimate 21-Day Guide to Increase your EQ, Improve your Social Skills and Communication at Work, and Master Your Emotions* will be covering the topic of optimism. This includes the "Law of "Attraction," the concept of optimism and its origins, and how to assure the "optimal" outcome for a given situation, especially a negative one. Optimism can be defined as the philosophical doctrine that this world must be the best (or most optimal) of all possible worlds and that the belief that good must ultimately prevail over evil in the universe. Of course, the concepts of good and evil can be fairly subjective. The basic ideas, though, are usually pretty straightforward for the most part. In this case, the concept of optimism will be used in the context of emotional intelligence and the knowledge and mastery of emotional awareness, assessment, understanding, and management. This is an extremely important part of mastering your emotions and raising your emotional intelligence and your emotional quotient, as a positive attitude and trust in the idea of optimism can be extremely helpful, and even vital, on one's journey to mastering their emotions, raising their emotional intelligence and emotional quotient, and ultimately beginning to live the most emotionally satisfying and fulfilling life possible.

The actual meaning of the word "optimism" comes from the French word "optimisme," which in turn, comes from the Latin term, "Optimum." This term translates to English as "best outcome" or "optimal." It reflects a belief that present and future conditions will work out for the best. For this reason, it is seen as a trait that encourages resilience in the face of stress. Research has shown that optimism can be reliably connected to positive results such as increased life expectancy, improved physical, mental, and emotional health increased success in work and social situations, greater recovery rates from physical conditions and traumatic events, and better-coping strategies when faced with and in response to adversity. Many individuals choose to view the concept of optimism as childish or unimportant. This, however, could not be further from reality. It may even be that an optimistic outlook is a default state for people to exist in, and as it can be a somewhat difficult state to maintain and manage successfully, gets lost later in life. If this is the case, and optimism is a trait that is possessed by us as children and simply gets lost later in life, then that could be a good explanation as to why some may view it as an inherently childish trait. This explanation would also serve to explain that a state of optimism is indeed something to strive for in adulthood, as a valuable skill that many seem to have forgotten in the midst of our regular day-to-day societal struggles.

With all that said and out of the way, today's actual assignment will be all about "reclaiming your childhood." In a literal sense, the actual goal for today's chapter of *The Ultimate 21-Day Guide to Increase your EQ, Improve your Social Skills and Communication at Work, and Master Your Emotions* will be to understand and gain a proper mastery of the concept and skill of optimism. In doing so, you will not only gain a more positive and self-beneficial attitude and outlook, but you will also begin the steps toward shedding the negative trait that replaces it over the course of our lives, which as I'm sure you may be aware, is referred to as pessimism. This is also often referred to as the "Glass Half Empty" attitude, as a counter to optimism's "Glass Half Full."

What you will want to do for today's assignment is to go about your day as normal. The only difference, as today's topic is more of a conceptual one, rather than an actual mission to complete, will be in an attitude adjustment of sorts. As you go about your day, you should be making an active attempt to keep in mind the concept of optimism and use the information covered earlier in this chapter to maintain an optimistic outlook. You should be considering the things talked about previously, on earlier days, as well. Pay especially close attention to your emotional states, and try to maintain this optimistic attitude if or when you happen to find yourself in a particularly difficult or uncomfortable situation.

You will also be using the "Law of Attraction," in order to help you accomplish today's task. The "Law of Attraction" is, put simply, the ability to attract into our lives whatever we may be focusing on. The law of attraction is a sort of extension of the concepts of optimism and pessimism. Basically, it states that if you focus on positive outcomes and remain optimistic, then positive outcomes will start to come your way as well. This may also sound somewhat farfetched, but it really can help those who believe in it. There is something about a positive attitude that fosters positivity in those in close proximity to it and the person behind it. This can also work in the opposite way, though, too. A negative attitude can attract negative outcomes by pushing others away or even through a sort of confirmation bias. This can be similar to the experience of having a particularly bad day and becoming more and more irritated as a result of completely mundane events. Paying attention to this sort of thing may even be connected to emotional awareness and assessment, the skills covered in the first two chapters of this book. As such, it will be a valuable part of mastering optimism, and in turn, taking one more step on the path to mastering your emotions and improving your emotional intelligence and emotional quotient.

Day 7:
Mastering Self-Control

During yesterday's chapter, the topics of optimism and the law of attraction were discussed. This is a valuable skill, as a belief that this world must be the best (or most optimal) of all possible worlds, and that the belief that good must ultimately prevail over evil in the universe, and that present and future conditions will work out for the best can be extremely helpful in mastering your emotions and raising your emotional intelligence and your emotional quotient. It may be difficult to accomplish some or even all of the goals to be set on today and the next 14 days' assignments if you are not sure of the apparent inclination of the world around you, and that things will balance out and work out for the best. How can you be expected to take this type of action in order to better yourself in the ways that are aimed for in *The Ultimate 21-Day Guide to Increase your EQ, Improve your Social Skills and Communication at Work, and Master Your Emotions*, if you are not literally confident enough to be sure of their eventual outcome once you have finished the book, after all?

However, today's chapter will be covering the topic of Self-control. This includes handling disruptive or intrusive emotions, and how to discern what they mean, as well as how to direct energy, especially negative energy. The skill of self-control can be defined as the ability to control oneself, in particular, one's emotions and desires or the expression of them in one's behavior, especially in difficult situations. Of course, the concepts of controlling your emotions and the expression of those emotions are, honestly, fairly straightforward. In this case, the concept of self-control will be used in the context of emotional intelligence and the knowledge and mastery of emotional awareness, assessment, understanding, and management. This is an extremely important part of mastering your emotions and raising your emotional intelligence and your emotional quotient, as self-control and discipline can be extremely helpful, and even vital, on one's journey to mastering their emotions, raising their emotional intelligence and emotional quotient, and ultimately beginning to live the most emotionally satisfying and fulfilling life possible. Additionally, this chapter will be a nice counter, or balance, to the last two days' chapters, which covered two inherently very positive concepts, in self-confidence and optimism. Following those with the lesson of self-control will be good for rounding out your progress on the way to mastering your emotional intelligence, and subsequently raising your emotional quotient, up to this point.

Self-control, or the ability to subdue one's impulses, emotions, and behaviors in order to achieve long-term goals, as a skill, is based strongly on one's level of emotional discipline. Many people believe that these concepts of discipline and self-control are actually the main factor that separates us, the modern people, from their ancestors and the rest of the animal kingdom. This makes perfect sense, as these traits come from the prefrontal cortex, which is significantly larger in humans than most, if not any other mammals with similarly structured brains. It is thanks to the prefrontal cortex that we do not simply respond immediately to any and all external stimuli, and can instead choose to evaluate and assess a situation in order to plan for the best possible outcome. This is, naturally, a valuable skill for those who may be seeking to increase their emotional intelligence and master their emotions.

With all of that said and out of the way, today's actual assignment will be all about raising your level of emotional discipline and improving your self-confidence. In doing so, the goal of today's chapter of *The Ultimate 21-Day Guide to Increase your EQ, Improve your Social Skills and Communication at Work, and Master Your Emotions* will be to gain a more refined and optimized method of action, by means of evaluating your current situation, understanding it, finding a path on which to act, and actually acting or responding. These four steps, of course, all mirror the tasks set for you in the first four days' chapters of this book. These skills will be useful in any and all future chapters based on skills that require taking active steps to master, as opposed to more conceptual ones.

What you will actually need to do for today's assignment is to use the skills referred to in the first four days' chapters of this book to gain a better understanding of self-control and discipline. As stated before, and as today's assignment is more is an actual mission that you will need to complete by taking active steps, you will be following the skeleton set on the first four days in order to complete it. The way to do so will be described below.

The first step to improving your levels of discipline and self-control is to use the skill of emotional awareness and emotional assessment to gain a proper understanding of the situation at hand in the present moment. The first step will be to become completely aware of the current situation and the emotional reactions you may have or want to feel. In order to do this, you will need to circle back to the first chapter and use the five levels of emotional awareness referred to in that chapter. The goal for this step will be to become completely aware of your current situation and the emotion or emotions it triggers within you. Of course, this can also be applied for the emotion or emotions of other individuals as well, in most cases. The next step will be to use this knowledge in order to evaluate, assess, and ultimately gain a complete understanding of the situation and its source or sources, as well as its significance and meanings, as described in the second day's chapter on emotional assessment.

The third step will be to use the knowledge gained from the first two steps in order to emotional assessment from the lesson on day two to take your emotional intelligence another step further. During this step, you will need to begin gauging your emotional needs, as described in the third day's chapter, with the context of emotional restraint in mind. During this step of gauging your emotional needs, you will need to do so in order to decide on a course of action that is appropriate for the situation. Sometimes, this may even take the form of inaction, and remaining passive in the present moment, until it becomes appropriate, at which point you may respond accordingly. Finally, the fourth and last step is actually the simplest, conceptually speaking. Of course, actually taking action may not be so simple. This will depend on the action you decided on taking during the third step, and may not even involve actually doing anything at all. However, once you have completed these steps, the task is done for now! Of course, these steps will be necessary to complete multiple times in a day, with as many difficult or trying situations as may occur, but once you understand how to handle these types of situations appropriately and with the necessary grace, you will have learned the tools necessary to use in all future endeavors moving forward.

Day 8:
Why Conscientiousness Matters

During yesterday's chapter of *Ultimate 21-Day Guide to Increase your EQ, Improve your Social Skills and Communication at Work, and Master Your Emotions*, the topic of self-control was discussed. This is a valuable skill, as handling disruptive or intrusive emotions, and how to discern what they mean, as well as how to direct energy, especially negative energy, can be extremely helpful in mastering your emotions and raising your emotional intelligence and your emotional quotient. It may be difficult to accomplish some or even all of the goals to be set on today's and the next 13 days' assignments if you do not have a good sense of control over your emotions, especially intrusive ones, your ability to discern their meanings, and how to properly direct them in a positive and appropriate manner. How can you be expected to take this type of action in order to better yourself, after all, in the ways that are aimed for in *The Ultimate 21-Day Guide to Increase your EQ, Improve your Social Skills and Communication at Work, and Master Your Emotions*, if you are not literally confident enough to do the work involved in the first place?

However, today's chapter will be covering the topic of conscientiousness. Conscientiousness can be defined as the quality of wishing to do one's work or duty well and thoroughly. This includes the ability to take responsibility for personal performance and owning your achievements as well as your mistakes. Gaining a good handle on this skill of conscientiousness can be difficult, as it can take very high levels of self-control and discipline. This is actually fortunate, as the last chapter covered the concept of self-control. Conscientiousness will be the last skill to be discussed in this section of *The Ultimate 21-Day Guide to Increase your EQ, Improve your Social Skills and Communication at Work, and Master Your Emotions* dedicated to "intrapersonal" skills. This is also an extremely important part of mastering your emotions and raising your emotional intelligence and your emotional quotient, as an owner of personal performance, achievements, and mistakes can be extremely helpful, and even vital, on one's journey to mastering their emotions, raising their emotional intelligence and emotional quotient, and ultimately beginning to live the most emotionally satisfying and fulfilling life possible.

Conscientiousness is all about how a person controls, regulates and directs their impulses. As such, it relates very heavily to a strong mastery of discipline and self-control. People with a high level of conscientiousness are able to form more long-term goals and constantly work in order to ensure success and achieve these goals, despite any adversity they may encounter. Additionally, most people typically consider individuals with a high level of mastery over the skill of conscientiousness to be very responsible and reliable. However, those who appear to display these traits can also tend to have obstructive habits, such as perfectionism or over-the-top workaholism. These sorts of traits can lead to things like burnout or exhaustion, and as such, may cause these same individuals to be perceived as boring, tired, or inflexible. As such, it is very important to keep your newly acquired skill of self-control to practice moderation alongside the mastery of conscientiousness, so as to avoid these sorts of negative habits and perceptions. If you can manage to do this properly, this should not be a concern.

With all of that said, though, today's actual assignment will be all about improving your skills of conscientiousness while maintaining a handle of the self-control learned in yesterday's chapter. This will also be good practice for those skills as well, which is very fortunate. This assignment for today's chapter will have you keep in mind and continue practicing the skills you will have learned during yesterday's chapter, of self-control and discipline. With these skills, you should be taking it one step further and adding in this new one. You should be actively taking responsibility for mistakes you make throughout the day, as well as your successes. Even before that, though, you will want to begin to practice using more goal-oriented behavior. This means that you should be setting both short and long-term goals for yourself, in order to accomplish them more successfully and more reliably. When you are assigned a task to complete, or when you find a new goal to complete, you should be making plans around it and set smaller milestones within the overall mission, in order to allow you to gauge your progress and to help you maintain motivation for much longer. In doing so, you will not only become a more conscientious person but a more organized and successful one as well. With these skills, you can help yourself to become more reliable and more responsible, and increasing your overall strength as a person as well as a more emotionally intelligent and self-aware one as well. With this, the current section of this book, covering "intrapersonal" skills, comes to a close, and you can move on to the next part. The next section of *The Ultimate 21-Day Guide to Increase your EQ, Improve your Social Skills and Communication at Work, and Master Your Emotions* will be about skills more suited for social interactions and helping you to become a more socially competent person, as well as allowing you to move yet another step closer to mastering your emotions and improving your social skills in your daily life and at work.

Day 9:
Increase Your Social Awareness

Congratulations! You have finished another section of *The Ultimate 21-Day Guide to Increase your EQ, Improve your Social Skills and Communication at Work, and Master Your Emotions*! You now have all of the tools necessary to understand and accomplish each of the 12 remaining days' tasks and goals, and are well on your way to completing this journey of personal growth and self-improvement. This section may be a little different from the first two, though. The first group covered the skills you needed in order to proceed with the rest of this book and set yourself up for success in mastering your emotional intelligence. The second was on a collection of "intrapersonal skills," which focused on improving yourself and mastering your own emotions. For this third section, however, you will have to change gears a little bit, and take a little turn off of that path. This section of the book will be helping you to improve your social skills.

With all of that said and out of the way, however, today's chapter will be going over the topic of social awareness. Social awareness can be defined as having an in-depth understanding of societal and communal set-ups, environments, problems, struggles, norms, and cultures, so as to allow yourself to feel the pulse and vibes of the society you are living in, as well as individuals around you. What this means is that, in more practical terms, social awareness is the ability to know and feel the people around you and the ability to interact with them in the most efficient and proper manner. In this case, the term "social awareness" will be used in the context of emotional intelligence and in relation to the emotional intelligence and knowledge and mastery of emotional awareness, assessment, understanding, and management. This is an extremely important part of mastering your emotions and raising your emotional intelligence and your emotional quotient, as it may be difficult to accomplish some or even all of the goals and tasks to be set on future days' assignments if you do not have a strong grasp of social awareness and the ability to perceive and understand the emotions of the people around you, as well as the ability to completely understand your surroundings and social contexts of difficult or trying situations. If you do not have a proper understanding and mastery of the skill of social awareness, after all, how can you be expected to properly master your emotions and become a more empathetic and emotionally intelligent person, enabling you to live the most fulfilling and emotionally satisfying life you can, as is aimed for in *The Ultimate 21-Day Guide to Increase your EQ, Improve your Social Skills and Communication at Work, and Master Your Emotions*?

Of course, just the term "social awareness" can be somewhat vague on its own. The actual assignment for today's chapter of *The Ultimate 21-Day Guide to Increase your EQ, Improve your Social Skills and Communication at Work, and Master Your Emotions* will be to use the skills learned in the first section of this book to parallel the first day's chapter on emotional awareness with the slightly altered context of being applied to social situations. This chapter will be applying these skills to other individuals and even larger groups of people. The actual steps to take in this chapter, as stated previously, will mirror the assignment from the first day's chapter. As such, it will follow the five levels of emotional awareness from that chapter as well.

If you are at the first level, you should be looking, during emotionally strenuous situations that may arise during the day, out for the physical reactions that the people around you may have in response to specific triggers. Consider why this is, and which emotions they are tied to.

If you fall under the second tier, the task will be to look out for your "action tendencies," and evaluate why the people involved in these situations would want to remove themselves, for example, and understand the emotional root is that these reactions are connected to.

For the third level of emotional awareness, the goal is to recognize emotional states as they occur from inciting external stimuli. Consider how other people may feel and react to specific events as they happen, and what sort of state they promote, emotionally. Try to understand how conflicting events might make people feel, and the various ranges of emotional reactions they may experience, both in nature as well as intensity.

For the fourth stage, you should be looking for situations throughout the day that elicit strong reactions from others around you. Try to gauge how they might feel in these scenarios and how they might react or feel in response. You should be attempting to go through the previous days again, while also considering the emotional states and reactions of other individuals.

Once you have reached the fifth, and last level of social awareness, you have reached the end and can exhibit a competent understanding of all of the skills talked about in this chapter. You should still be taking these skills into consideration during daily life, however, as they are not ones that can always be mastered in just a few days. Practice does make perfect, after all, and you should always be striving to better yourself in any and every way that you can.

Day 10:
How To Develop Your Empathy

Today, as the second part of the "social skills" section of *The Ultimate 21-Day Guide to Increase your EQ, Improve your Social Skills and Communication at Work and Master Your Emotions,* we will cover a concept that is very similar and connected to what you learned about in yesterday's chapter. This assignment will be covering the topic of empathy, rather than simply being socially aware. The best way to think about and understand the idea of empathy in relation to social awareness is as an extension of that concept, rather than its own separate idea. Naturally, the next step after acknowledging and becoming aware of the emotional states of those around you would be to consider then and gain a proper understanding of those emotions.

Empathy is the second part of this section designed to give you the tools necessary to increase your social skills at home and work, and ultimately grow as a person and maximize your potential for emotional intelligence as well as your EQ. Empathy can be defined as the ability to acknowledge, understand, and share the feelings of another person. What this means is that once you have begun to gain an awareness of the emotional states of those around you, you can also begin to Learn to take an active interest in others' emotional states, as well as how to recognize and anticipate others' needs by sensing and intuiting their responses to stimuli. This skill will be very important down the road, as simply acknowledging and recognizing people's emotions will not allow you to do very much, unless you also have the ability to know where these sorts of emotions come from, what they mean on a deeper level, and what to do about them as they arise. Additionally, social awareness can be a valuable tool for pushing your emotional intelligence (as well as your emotional quotient) even further. Future goals to be completed over the following days will also rely on a solid understanding and mastery over this skill and the ones that are associated with it.

As far as the actual meaning of the word "empathy," a more detailed definition of the word would be that empathy is "the experience of understanding another person's thoughts, feelings, and condition from his or her point of view, rather than from one's own." It facilitates social or helpful behaviors that come from within, rather than being forced, to ensure that people behave in a more compassionate manner. The concept of empathy also differs from sympathy in multiple very distinct ways. Sympathy is about feeling sadness or pity for someone who is undergoing some type of hardship. In other words, sympathy is when a person receives some sort of emotional reaction on behalf of another person, often without even considering how that person may actually feel or respond to that particular situation. Empathy, on the other hand, promotes selfless compassion and action on behalf of another person or group of people based on their own emotional reaction or reactions. While this initially sounds preferable and much more considerate, studies have shown that having an excessively high level of empathy can be detrimental to one's own health and interfere with decision-making or cloud your judgment. As such, today's assignment will be another one during which it will be important to continue practicing self-control in order to avoid pushing your empathic responses too far and letting it become an unhealthy habit.

As far as the actual assignment for today goes, you will need to spend time throughout the day using the skills of social awareness covered in yesterday's chapter, combined with the lessons from the first two days as well, to improve your level of empathy. As you make progress with these skills, you should also be making an effort to consider why you and the people around you react in the ways that you do, and why which of your emotional responses occur as a result to which external triggers. What are the root causes behind these emotional reactions, and what do they mean. Why do some specific external triggers elicit stronger or milder responses from the people around you? How would or do those people around you feel about or even react to a specific situation? You should be asking questions similar to these ones that relate to the current day's tasks and lessons. The important thing is to be asking why, in regards to your emotional states and reactions, and considering them in terms of their origins and how to handle them now as well as in the future.

Are you enjoying the book so far? If so, I would really appreciate if you could take a moment to leave a short review on Amazon. Thank you, it means a lot to me!

Day 11:
The Keys of Effective Communication

The assignment from yesterday was all about using your newfound skills of social awareness and empathy to begin to understand and assess the emotional states of the people around you, as well as their meanings and origins. Today's lesson will be taking that idea and pushing it another step further. This chapter will be about using those skills to cultivate new ones to help you to communicate effectively to others. This communication, for the sake of this lesson, will be in the context of the emotions of yourself and the people around you. Naturally, it will also be applicable for other people, as this section of *The Ultimate 21-Day Guide to Increase your EQ, Improve your Social Skills and Communication at Work, and Master Your Emotions* is about improving your social skills and becoming more socially competent.

Communicating effectively will require you to use your knowledge of emotional and social awareness, as well as the newly learned skill of empathy, in order to begin to understand how to communicate these emotions and their meanings with others effectively. You will need to pay particularly close attention to the "action tendencies" from the second stage of emotional awareness, which this book talked about in its first chapter. What it actually means to communicate effectively with other people around you is to use the knowledge of your action tendencies and emotional awareness as a whole, as well as the things you might learn during an assessment of a person's emotional states and their meanings, to actually understand them and what they signify for whichever individual may be experiencing these emotions in a particular moment, and accurately express this information to the person or people it may be relevant or applicable for. Additionally, a good mastery of this skill will allow you or others to help other individuals to understand their emotions and emotional states, their meanings, and what they might actually need to do in response to these emotions. It can also be useful in helping people to understand what they will need to do moving forward when they experience these types of emotions in response to external stimuli in the future, or even how to predict and prevent negative ones from occurring in the future. This will help you to assist others in understanding how to solve any problems that they may encounter. It will also be a vital step on the way to your goals of mastering your emotions and improving your emotional intelligence and emotional quotient, as you can't take effective action to solve these sorts of problems and rectify difficult or problematic situations unless you have a complete and proper understanding of what the problem is and how to actually fix or handle it once you do gain this sort of understanding.

Today's assignment will be to use the skills of social and emotional awareness and assessment to take your emotional intelligence yet another step further. Today, you will begin to use the knowledge gained during the steps of acknowledging and analyzing the emotions and emotional states of others in order to communicate effectively with them. The goal for today's assignment will be to keep these sorts of reactions and their causes and meanings in mind to consider the best way to communicate effectively with those they apply to. It may be difficult, however, to communicate effectively in this way before properly understanding how to do so. As such, there will be a few things to keep in mind as a guide when attempting to communicate with others in regards to the emotions and emotional states that you or they may be experiencing, listed below.

The first thing to consider when attempting to effectively communicate with others regarding emotional states that you or they may experience is that you should always be taking their feelings and emotions into account, before anything else. You should always be asking why things are the way they are. If a person tells you some sort of secret or something that they may wish to hide because they trust you as a friend, for example, you should always try to be aware of this and proceed accordingly. This might not even always be related to you or things you have done, either. Sometimes a person may act angry or irritated with you, when the problem is not, in fact, something that you caused, and they are not actually upset with you. This is very important to consider and can be vital if you may be trying to help that person through the current situation.

The second thing to keep in mind, and the other side of this coin, is that you should also be aware of your own emotions when communicating with other individuals. Just as another person's feelings can have an impact on the messages that they may be trying to send, your own feelings and emotions can get in the way of your communication, as well. When you experience a strong emotion or feeling, pay attention to that emotion and try not to let it get in the way of your message. Both positive emotions, like happiness, and negative emotions, like anger, can affect how we communicate in this way. For example, if you are really happy about something, or even tired or exhausted, you may agree to do things that you should not or would not typically agree to under normal circumstances. On the other hand, if you are angry, you might say something mean to someone who has nothing to do with your current emotional state. When you have a good understanding of your own feelings and emotions, you will notice these emotions and it will become much easier to prevent them from getting in the way of your communication.

The third and last note to be discussed here will be that in order to communicate effectively regarding your emotions and emotional states and those of the people around you, is exactly what the last chapter of this book was about. You need to remain empathetic! You can't expect to effectively and consistently communicate thoughts or concepts regarding emotions and emotional states if you do not actually understand those emotions in the first place. For example, if you notice that a coworker seems stressed, you should make some sort of attempt to find out why. If she tells you she is stressed out because she does not have a lot of time to finish a big project, you can empathize with her by putting yourself in her shoes. That means, you can imagine yourself in this situation and you can understand what that person must be feeling. When you have empathy for a person, you can think about how you would want to be talked to or what you would like other people to say or do if you were in that situation, or how you would prefer for the situation to be handled. Going back to the example with your coworker, you could offer to help your coworker with the project or offer some words of encouragement, provided that you believe they would appreciate the gesture.

With all of that said, you should have all of the tools necessary to complete today's assignment and take another step on the path to self-improvement and mastering your emotions. Using the skills you learned previously, as with all assignments, will help you to ensure your success in this and all of the future chapters. Keeping this in mind, today's lesson should also be helpful, once it has been completed, for the assignments to come from the remaining days in this 21-day guide to improving your social skills and increasing your level of emotional intelligence.

Day 12:
Forming Positive And Meaningful Bonds With Other People

The assignment from yesterday was all about using your newfound skills of social awareness and empathy to begin to understand, assess, and effectively communicate with regards to the emotional states of the people around you, as well as their meanings and origins. Today's lesson will be somewhat separate from yesterday's chapter, but not completely so. This chapter will be about using those skills to cultivate new ones in order to help you in forming lasting and meaningful bonds with other people. These skills, for the sake of this lesson, will be in the context of and keeping in mind the emotions of yourself and the people around you, as the basis for healthy and mutually beneficial and positive interpersonal relationships. Naturally, it will also be applicable for other people, as this section of *The Ultimate 21-Day Guide to Increase your EQ, Improve your Social Skills and Communication at Work, and Master Your Emotions* is about improving your social skills and becoming more socially competent.

Forming positive and meaningful bonds with other individuals can be a very important skill to learn. Many people say, after all, that humans are primarily social creatures. Connecting with other individuals is at the heart of human nature, and as such, is a very large part of a successful, satisfying, and fulfilling life. It can help to improve our creativity, our physical, mental, and emotional resilience, and even our life expectancy. It is, however, very easy for us to get caught up in our daily struggles and begin to overlook these sorts of connections. It is becoming easier and easier every day to fall victim to the tight pressures of work life, deadlines, and the increasingly alarming rate of technological advancement, which can all leave us struggling to keep up on a day-to-day basis. For these reasons, it may be more crucial than ever to emphasize the importance of forming meaningful bonds with others, in order to maximize your potential for social skills and live a more emotionally fulfilling life.

Forming meaningful bonds and friendships will require you to use your knowledge of emotional and social awareness, as well as the newly learned skill of effective communication, in order to build meaningful relationships with individuals or groups of other people. You will need to pay particularly close attention to the knowledge and insight gained from the skills used in the previous chapters from the section of this book on social skills, which include social awareness, empathy, and communication. What it actually means to form these kinds of meaningful bonds with other people around you is to use the knowledge of a person's emotional responses and patterns, along with their action tendencies, as well as the newly acquired social skills from this section of the book in order to connect with other individuals.

As far as the actual assignment goes, you will need to actually take the steps described above in order to form new connections with people throughout the day. There are a number of ways to accomplish this, of course. One method of which is to find a common goal or interest. Sharing in a mutual goal with another person or people can create a sort of bonding experience that's based on a positive support system, which is a healthy way to build upon a relationship with friends or loved ones. This can take many different forms, including things like a shared fitness goal, working on a professional project together, or even something simple like planning to cut down on television watch-time or creating a diet plan.

Another method to assist you in forming important and meaningful bonds will be to make some sort of social plans. A day trip, maybe, if it is someone you are already familiar with. It might be good to share a meal with the person you are trying to get to know. Sharing a meal with someone can be an excellent way to get to know them better. Eating with someone is a bonding experience as old as the human experience. We care more for those with whom we've shared meals. It might even be sufficient to do something as simple and passive as sharing a common space with a person. Occupying the same shared space can subconsciously make people feel more comfortable in itself. Anywhere with defined borders can be seen as intimate, and serve to make the people inside that space feel more comfortable with it and each other, enforcing a positive relationship and encouraging the types of bonds that are being aimed for in today's assignment.

A third method, and the last to be listed here, for enforcing positive relationships and helping to form meaningful bonds and friendships with other people, is based simply on common sense. This method is to simply express kindness to the person you wish to get to know better. Something as simple as offering to help with a difficult task or goal can work well, regardless of how well you know this person. Even small gestures here and there can be sufficient. It does not have to be a large, grand gesture in order to work in this way. The important thing here is to think of what might help the other person the most and act accordingly.

Obviously, there are many more methods to assist you in accomplishing this task. If needed, you can be as creative as you see fit. The methods listed are just a few simple ideas. With all of that said, you should have all of the tools necessary to complete today's assignment and take another step on the path to self-improvement and mastering your emotions. Using the skills you learned previously, as with all assignments, will help you to ensure your success in this and all of the future chapters. Keeping this in mind, today's lesson should also be helpful, once it has been completed, for the assignments to come from the remaining days in this 21-day guide to improving your social skills and increasing your level of emotional intelligence.

Day 13:
How To Build And Maintain Trust

The assignment from yesterday was all about using your newfound skills of social awareness, empathy, and communication to cultivate new ones in order to help you in forming lasting and meaningful bonds with other people. Today's lesson will be slightly different and separate from yesterday's chapter, but not completely so. This chapter will be about Developing and Maintaining standards of honesty and integrity, and learning to use effective methods to assure others These skills, for the sake of this lesson, will be in the context of and keeping in mind the emotions of yourself and the people around you, as the basis for healthy and mutually beneficial and positive interpersonal relationships. Naturally, it will also be applicable for other people, as this section of *The Ultimate 21-Day Guide to Increase your EQ, Improve your Social Skills and Communication at Work, and Master Your Emotions* is about improving your social skills and becoming more socially competent.

Learning how to build trust and enforce the bonds formed during yesterday's assignment effectively will require you to use your knowledge of emotional and social awareness, as well as the newly learned skill of empathy, communication, and forming bonds, in order to begin to build trust with new acquaintances, as well as one friends and coworkers. You will need to pay particularly close attention to the emotions and emotional reactions of other people, which you can discern using the skills of social awareness and empathy, as discussed in previous chapters. Of course, you can circle back to those chapters as needed, if you feel a little bit rusty on the topics they covered.

What it really means to build trust with people you know is to communicate effectively and remain empathetic toward those people in order to understand their emotional needs and provide reassurance or show them that they can rely on and depend on you when they are in need. Additionally, a good mastery of this skill will help you even further in forming initial bonds with new acquaintances and develop strong friendships all on its own, in some specific contexts. Most likely, you will need to combine it with previously learned skills, such as empathy, social awareness, and the ones covered in the last chapter. Building trust, especially in new acquaintances and friends, can even make it easier to provide them with assistance, as they will be more willing to accept it from someone they are already familiar with and trust, even to a slight degree. It can also help you in providing many different forms of emotional support or boosting their moods and emotional states in difficult or uncomfortable situations. It will also be a vital step on the way to your goals of mastering your emotions and improving your emotional intelligence and emotional quotient, as you can't take effective action to solve these sorts of problems and rectify difficult or problematic situations unless you have a complete and proper understanding of what the problem is and how to actually fix or handle it once you do gain this sort of understanding.

As for the actual assignment for today's chapter of *The Ultimate 21-Day Guide to Increase your EQ, Improve your Social Skills and Communication at Work, and Master Your Emotions*, you will need to use the previously learned skills of empathy and building bonds to build trust and further support your interpersonal relationships with other individuals, and in turn, take your overall emotional intelligence another step further. The actual goal for today's assignment will be to keep these sorts of concepts and ideas, as well as the rest of the skills covered in this "social skills" section in mind to consider the best way to communicate effectively and build or enforce positive bonds with the people around you. It may be difficult, however, to communicate effectively in this way before properly understanding how to do so. A good method to consider when attempting to build trust and reinforce bonds between yourself and other friends or acquaintances is honesty. This one shouldn't require much of a response, as it is a fairly straightforward concept. Being completely honest is a great way to display trustworthiness, as it involves transparency and a lack of deception. When you can be sure that someone will not lie to you, or that they will even simply be honest with you and communicate what they are thinking or feeling accurately and truthfully, will go miles on the road toward building a good sense of trust. As such, this will be the assignment for today. You will need to exhibit total honesty with the people around you in order to build trust and encourage the reinforcement of new and existing bonds. This not only includes the absence of lies or deception but total transparency. You should also be attempting to avoid hiding things or keeping secrets about yourself. You do not necessarily need to explain every embarrassing quirk about yourself to everyone you meet and know, but everyone has moments during the day during which they think to themselves that a certain thought they might have or that specific detail about themselves is not worth sharing. During these sorts of moments, you should try to be more forthcoming with these sorts of thoughts. Obviously, there are some that might not be vital to the conversation, or very constructive, and those may not be necessary to reveal, and you can definitely use your best judgment on this assignment, as with all others. However, the goal is to be more honest, and this includes being honest with yourself. That's the most important thing to consider, is that you should be aiming to be more honest with yourself and others, and the goal is self-improvement. You should always be striving to improve, no matter what.

With all of that said, you should have all of the tools necessary to complete today's assignment and take another step on the path to self-improvement and mastering your emotions. Using the skills you learned previously, as with all assignments, will help you to ensure your success in this and all of the future chapters. Keeping this in mind, today's lesson should also be helpful, once it has been completed, for the assignments to come from the remaining days in this 21-day guide to improving your social skills and increasing your level of emotional intelligence.

Day 14:
Working Together To Accomplish A Common Goal

The assignment from yesterday's chapter of *The Ultimate 21-Day Guide to Increase your EQ, Improve your Social Skills and Communication at Work, and Master Your Emotions* covered the concept of trustworthiness, and instructed on how to build trust through openness and total honesty effectively. This chapter will be on a topic which is somewhat connected to those concepts, which is teamwork. You will be working on your skills of collaboration and cooperation in order to Learn to work alongside others toward shared goals and use effective leadership strategies to maintain environments conducive to accomplishing goals and maximizing positive emotional states. These skills, for the sake of this lesson, will be in the context of and keeping in mind the emotions of yourself and the people around you, as the basis for healthy and positive interpersonal relationships. Naturally, it will also be applicable for other people, as this section of *The Ultimate 21-Day Guide to Increase your EQ, Improve your Social Skills and Communication at Work, and Master Your Emotions* is about improving your social skills and becoming more socially competent.

This chapter of *The Ultimate 21-Day Guide to Increase your EQ, Improve your Social Skills and Communication at Work, and Master Your Emotions* will help you in learning to use the social skills of social awareness, empathy, communication, forming bonds, and building trust in order to work effectively with other people to accomplish a common goal. It will be important to use these skills, as trust and effective communication, as with the other social skills, and even the skills learned in earlier chapters, can be essential to working well with other people. As such, you will need to pay particularly close attention to the skills of empathy and communication. When working cooperatively with other people, it is important to pay attention to their feelings and emotions, in order to maintain equilibrium and efficiency. Of course, you can circle back to previous chapters as needed, if you feel a little bit rusty on the topics they covered.

What it really means to work effectively in a team with other people you know is to communicate effectively, build trust, and practice empathy with those people in order to understand their emotional needs, provide assistance, or show them that they can rely on and depend on you when they are in need in order to form meaningful bonds and promote synergy and cooperation. Additionally, a good mastery of this skill will help you even further in forming positive social bonds with new acquaintances and develop strong friendships all on its own, in some situations. You will need to combine it with previously learned skills, such as empathy, social awareness, and the ones covered in the last chapter. Building trust, especially in new acquaintances and friends, can even make it easier to provide them with assistance, as they will be more willing to accept it from someone they are already familiar with and who they trust, even to a slight degree. This can help you in providing many different forms of emotional support or boosting their moods and emotional states in difficult or uncomfortable situations. It will also be a vital step on the way to your goals of mastering your emotions and improving your emotional intelligence and emotional quotient, as you can't take effective action to solve and rectify difficult or problematic situations unless you have a complete and proper understanding of what the problem is and how to actually fix or handle it once you do gain this sort of understanding.

An important thing to consider during this assignment is that people are both the trouble and the reason with and for creating better and more effective and efficient teamwork. What this means is that, no matter what a group's nature or purpose is, each person involved will always carry their own skills and quirks. Sometimes these can be difficult or frustrating to manage, but diversity in life and work experience, personalities, and skill sets can also be very beneficial in constructing a good team of individuals and ultimately be the key factor in effective teamwork. As such, the goal for today's chapter will be to use your knowledge of emotional states and reactions, as well as the skills of empathy and communication in order to understand other individuals and the qualities they bring to a team or group. What are their strengths? What are their weaknesses? Do they have any interesting quirks or life experience that may be relevant?

Additionally, you should be considering how to handle those qualities in these people, and how to communicate with them so as to best promote synergy in a group setting. This assignment is more of a conceptual one, based on thought and contemplation rather than taking action, but these are all important factors to consider in a collaborative setting. Understanding the important qualities, both tools, and quirks, about other people and yourself, is the key to understanding how to create an effective and efficient team of individuals and will set you up for success in collaborative and even in leadership-based roles in the future.

With all of that said, you should have all of the tools necessary to complete today's assignment and take another step on the path to self-improvement and mastering your emotions. Using the skills you learned previously, as with all assignments, will help you to ensure your success in this and all of the future chapters. Keeping this in mind, today's lesson should also be helpful, once it has been completed, for the assignments to come from the remaining days in this 21-day guide to improving your social skills and increasing your level of emotional intelligence.

Day 15:
Resolving Conflicts

The assignment from yesterday's chapter of *The Ultimate 21-Day Guide to Increase your EQ, Improve your Social Skills and Communication at Work, and Master Your Emotions* covered the concepts of teamwork, collaboration, and cooperation, and instructed on how to effectively promote synergy and evaluate the qualities relevant to these sorts of situations. This chapter will be on the somewhat connected, if not slightly removed topic, of conflict resolution. You will be using your newly acquired skills of collaboration and cooperation in order to gain a deeper understanding of how to work effectively with groups of other people by understanding and solving potential issues as they arise. If you have a strong enough grasp of this skill, you might even be able to anticipate and prevent these types of issues before they even occur. These skills, for the sake of this lesson, will be in the context of and keeping in mind the emotions of yourself and the people around you, as the basis for healthy and positive interpersonal relationships. Naturally, it will also be applicable for other people, as this section of *The Ultimate 21-Day Guide to Increase your EQ, Improve your Social Skills and Communication at Work, and Master Your Emotions* is about improving your social skills and becoming more socially competent.

This chapter of *The Ultimate 21-Day Guide to Increase your EQ, Improve your Social Skills and Communication at Work, and*

Master Your Emotions will help you in learning to use the social skills of social awareness, empathy, communication, forming bonds, and building trust in order to work effectively with other people to settle differences and ultimately understand one another better. These skills can become crucial when working in group-oriented and collaborative projects. As such, you will need to pay particularly close attention to the skills of empathy and communication. When working cooperatively with other people, it is important to keep in mind their feelings and emotions in order to maintain efficiency and equilibrium. Of course, you are allowed to circle back to previous chapters as needed, if you feel that it might be necessary or that you could be a little bit rusty on the topics they covered and their daily goals.

Conflict resolution is a way for two or more individuals or groups of people to find a peaceful and ideally mutually, beneficial solution to a disagreement among them. When a dispute arises, the best course of action is usually to use tactics of negotiation to resolve the issue immediately, or even anticipate the issue in order to prevent it beforehand. The actual goals of successful negotiations are to help all parties involved to find equilibrium and peace amongst themselves and each other and improve relationships between people and their understandings of each other's feelings and emotions. Conflict resolution through negotiation can be good for all parties involved. Often, each side will get more by participating in negotiations than they would by walking away, and it can be a way for your group to get resources that might otherwise be out of reach. This sort of conflict resolution can help you to understand more about other people whose ideas, beliefs, or backgrounds may be different from your own. In order to resolve a conflict, you will need to look at the situation from the point of view of all parties involved and learn more about these people's perspectives and motivations. Additionally, learning how to effectively resolve conflicts can be helpful in ensuring that your relationships with acquaintances can be a vital step on the way to your goals of mastering your emotions and improving your emotional intelligence and emotional quotient.

As far as the actual task for today's chapter of *The Ultimate 21-Day Guide to Increase your EQ, Improve your Social Skills and Communication at Work, and Master Your Emotions* goes, you will need to spend time throughout the day. You will be using the skills of awareness, assessment, and resolution from the first day's chapter to understand and figure out how to properly rectify interpersonal conflicts. If a situation arises for which it may actually be necessary to take action to rectify and resolve an issue between or among other people, you should try to take the initiative and attempt to step in, if you find it appropriate. Of course, this would be something to do after, and only after you have taken the time to consider the feelings and emotions of all parties involved, as well as the needs of those people and their significance to the sale of the group's collective well-being, both in the short- and long-term sense.

With all of that said, you should have all of the tools necessary to complete today's assignment and take another step on the path to self-improvement and mastering your emotions. Using the skills you learned previously, as with all assignments, will help you to ensure your success in this and all of the future chapters. Keeping this in mind, today's lesson should also be helpful, once it has been completed, for the assignments to come from the remaining days in this 21-day guide to improving your social skills and increasing your level of emotional intelligence.

Day 16:
How To Become Adaptable

During yesterday's chapter of *The Ultimate 21-Day Guide to Increase your EQ, Improve your Social Skills and Communication at Work, and Master Your Emotions*, the topic of conflict resolution was discussed. This is a valuable skill, as a complete understanding of how to work effectively with groups of other people by understanding and solving potential issues as they arise can be extremely helpful in mastering your emotions and raising your emotional intelligence and your emotional quotient. These skills, for the sake of this lesson, will be in the context of and keeping in mind the emotions of yourself and the people around you, as the basis for healthy and positive interpersonal relationships. Naturally, it will also be applicable for other people, as this section of *The Ultimate 21-Day Guide to Increase your EQ, Improve your Social Skills and Communication at Work, and Master Your Emotions* is about improving your social skills and becoming more socially competent.

This chapter of *The Ultimate 21-Day Guide to Increase your EQ, Improve your Social Skills and Communication at Work, and Master Your Emotions* will help you in learning to use some of the skills you will have acquired during the past days' assignments to help you in becoming a more adaptable and emotionally rounded and whole individual. These skills can become crucial when working in the types of dynamic, variable, and fast-paced environments that are so common in today's work-centric society. As such, you will need to pay particularly close attention to the skills you learned in the first four days of this book's journey to emotional mastery, as well as those from the chapters centered on the concepts of self-confidence, optimism, and self-control. When attempting to become a more emotionally flexible and adaptable person, it is important to keep in mind that, while it can be very easy to overlook adaptability as a skill to be sought after, it is an extremely vital aspect of becoming emotionally intelligent and socially adept. Of course, you are allowed to circle back to previous chapters as needed, if you feel that it might be necessary or that you could be a little bit rusty on the topics they covered and their daily goals.

Adaptability, as a concept, can be an important aspect of emotional intelligence. The quality of being flexible and open to new or unfamiliar situations and ideas can help to increase your emotional intelligence and emotional quotient and to help you become a more emotionally rounded individual. Develop the skills and ability to adapt to new situations can be very important both at work and in your personal life. New ideas and concept can be introduced every now and then, sometimes seemingly out of the blue. How you handle these types of situations can have very significant impacts on the overall outcome of the situation with regards to your own internal emotional states, as well as in an external sense. If a tense situation is handled poorly by even one person, especially if that person can be particularly expressive, it can throw off the balance of everyone involved as well as the situation itself.

As has been explained previously, the ability to remain adaptable and flexible to new or unexpected situations or events can be vital in especially tense or difficult ones. Fortunately, adaptability is a natural skill that all people already possess, at least to some degree. It is a skill that can be developed and mastered with practice, as well. A good way to actually work on improving your adaptability would be to have an accurate view and perception of the events as they occur. You should be actively observing your environment in order to be aware of the events around you. You might not be able to see the need for a change until you begin to actively pay attention to your surroundings. You should be trying, today and in the future as well, to be monitoring trends, attitudes, behaviors, and their causes and meanings as well. Use this information to compare present factors with past observations, and find out what has changed, or what hasn't, and why this might be.

Another method to increase your capacity for adaptability would be to simply be actively willing to learn. Simply observing your surroundings may not always be enough. If the result of these observations suggests that you may need to reach out for more information, you should absolutely be doing so. You should always be trying to learn and improve, no matter what. Some things can be learned on your own, provided you have sufficient resources to help you do so. However, some particularly difficult topics might require that you seek help from another source. You should never decline the help or services of another person if it would help you. You should also be taking action in response to the information you have learned from these steps. You should be attempting to integrate the skills covered in the first four chapters of this book, which involve acknowledging, understanding, and taking action in response to specific events. It is necessary to take action regarding the information you have learned about a situation that you need to adapt to. These adaptations will be all the more effective when the necessary action is taken as well. Lastly, you should be keeping in mind that some things will simply be out of your control, and that change is bound to occur regardless of the opinions of those affected. The best we can do is to adapt to these developments and try to improve ourselves as much as we can.

With all of that said, you should have all of the tools necessary to complete today's assignment and take another step on the path to self-improvement and mastering your emotions. Using the skills you learned previously, as with all assignments, will help you to ensure your success in this and all of the future chapters. Keeping this in mind, today's lesson should also be helpful, once it has been completed, for the assignments to come from the remaining days in this 21-day guide to improving your social skills and increasing your level of emotional intelligence.

Day 17:
What Is Innovativeness And How To Master It

During yesterday's chapter of *The Ultimate 21-Day Guide to Increase your EQ, Improve your Social Skills and Communication at Work, and Master Your Emotions*, the topic of adaptability was discussed. This is a valuable skill, as the ability to remain flexible and open to new or unfamiliar situations and ideas can be extremely helpful in mastering your emotions and raising your emotional intelligence and your emotional quotient. These skills, for the sake of today's assignment and its goals, will be discussed in the context of and keeping in mind the emotions of yourself and the people around you, as the basis for healthy and positive interpersonal relationships. Naturally, it will also be applicable for other people, as this section of *The Ultimate 21-Day Guide to Increase your EQ, Improve your Social Skills and Communication at Work, and Master Your Emotions* is about improving your social skills and becoming more socially competent.

This chapter might be a little bit different, however. During this lesson, the book will begin to shift into the last section of this book. Whereas the last section explained and aimed to guide you on the road to mastering a group of skills based on social interactions, the next one will be about topics that are more closely aligned with self-improvement and creativity. The topics to be covered in this section are innovativeness, initiating change, building and maintaining a sense of drive, striving for excellence and aiming to improve, and accepting the things that we cannot change. The first chapter of this last section of our journey to increase our emotional intelligence and emotional quotient, improve our social skills, and ultimately master our emotions will be on the topic of innovativeness, or the skill of learning to state new ideas and concepts, and to speak out about said concepts. This is somewhat of a counter or inverse to the concept of adaptability. Innovativeness, combined with the skills to be covered in the next chapters, will be helping you in self-improvement and betterment. This chapter is a little bit different, though, as it is also connected to the last section as a sort of inverse to the topic of adaptability.

This chapter of *The Ultimate 21-Day Guide to Increase your EQ, Improve your Social Skills and Communication at Work, and Master Your Emotions* will help you in learning to use some of the skills you will have acquired during the past days' assignments to help you in becoming a more innovative and creative individual. These skills can become crucial when working in the types of dynamic, variable, and fast-paced environments that are so common in today's work-centric society. As such, you will need to pay particularly close attention to the skills you learned in the first four days of this book's journey to emotional mastery, as well as those from the chapters centered on the concepts of self-confidence, optimism, and self-control. When attempting to become a more emotionally flexible and innovative person, it is important to keep in mind that, while it can be very easy to overlook adaptability and innovativeness as valuable skills to be sought after, they are extremely vital aspects of becoming emotionally intelligent and socially adept. Of course, you are allowed to circle back to previous chapters as needed, if you feel that it might be necessary or that you could be a little bit rusty on the topics they covered and their daily goals.

Innovativeness, much like adaptability, can be an important aspect of further developing and improving your emotional intelligence. The quality of being flexible and open to new or unfamiliar situations and ideas can help to increase your emotional intelligence and emotional quotient and to help you become a more emotionally rounded individual. Develop the skills and ability to adapt to new situations can be very important both at work and in your personal life. New ideas and concept can be introduced every now and then, sometimes seemingly out of the blue. How you handle these types of situations can have very significant impacts on the overall outcome of the situation with regards to your own internal emotional states, as well as in an external sense. If a tense situation is handled poorly by even one person, especially if that person can be particularly expressive, it can throw off the balance of everyone involved as well as the situation itself.

Innovativeness can also be very different, and even almost opposite to the concept of adaptability as well. Whereas being adaptable involves reacting in an appropriate manner to unexpected or unfamiliar situations, innovativeness is more about creating new situations in order to bring change. It is a much more active role, which can be thought of as the ability to mix things up, or to be spontaneous. This can be an important skill to learn because coming up with new and original ideas can help you to stand out from the crowd. Some of these ideas may even afford you better opportunities or other forms of positive consequences or results.

Fortunately, innovativeness is much like adaptability in that it is a skill that can be developed and mastered with practice, as well. A good way to actually work on improving this skill, much like with the skill of being adaptable, is to simply be willing to change. Most people can think of newer or more efficient ways to accomplish various tasks and goals. However, change takes energy, discipline, and a willingness to change for the sake of originality. Many of the activities designed to help us improve have a bit of a learning curve, and will take time to adjust to. If we switch from a method we've mastered to a new process of accomplishing a specific goal, we will always tend to be a little bit awkward at first. It always takes time and practice for us to return to our "normal" level of skill, but over time the value of this change will become clear, as we begin to improve and even move beyond our previous level of skill. This willingness to change is often driven by a fearless loyalty to doing what's right for the organization and customer, and will ultimately serve us better in the long run. The actual assignment for today, as such, will be to spend time thinking of out-of-the-box solutions to problems or unfamiliar situations that may arise throughout the day. You should be actively thinking of new and original solutions to these problems, and trying new ways to accomplish regular goals. The primary goal should be to improve.

With all of that said, you should have all of the tools necessary to complete today's assignment and take another step on the path to self-improvement and mastering your emotions. Using the skills you learned previously, as with all assignments, will help you to ensure your success in this and all of the future chapters. Keeping this in mind, today's lesson should also be helpful, once it has been completed, for the assignments to come from the remaining days in this 21-day guide to improving your social skills and increasing your level of emotional intelligence.

Day 18:
Initiate Change In Your Environment

Congratulations! You have now completely finished another section of *The Ultimate 21-Day Guide to Increase your EQ, Improve your Social Skills and Communication at Work, and Master Your Emotions*! This one was a little weird, as it was more of a slight transition between the sections. Yesterday's chapter was sort of between the "social skills" and this section, which is primarily about self-improvement. Regardless, you now have all of the tools necessary to understand and accomplish each of the remaining days' tasks and goals, and are well on your way to completing this journey of personal growth and self-improvement. This section may be a little different from the first three, though. The first group covered the skills you needed in order to proceed with the rest of this book and set yourself up for success in mastering your emotional intelligence. The second and third ones were a collection of "intrapersonal" and "interpersonal" skills, which focused on improving yourself and mastering your own emotions and those of the people around you. For this fourth section, however, you will have to change gears a bit again. This section of the book will be explaining why self-improvement should be a constant goal to strive for every day, and how you can put yourself in positions that will allow you to better yourself.

During yesterday's chapter of *The Ultimate 21-Day Guide to Increase your EQ, Improve your Social Skills and Communication at Work, and Master Your Emotions*, the topics of adaptability and innovativeness were discussed. These are valuable skills, as the abilities to remain flexible and open to new or unfamiliar situations, as well as the ability to actively form new and original ideas and solutions can be extremely helpful in mastering your emotions and raising your emotional intelligence and your emotional quotient. These skills, for the sake of today's assignment and its goals, will be discussed in the context of and keeping in mind the emotions of yourself and the people around you, as the basis for healthy and positive interpersonal relationships. Naturally, it will also be applicable for other people, as this section of The *Ultimate 21-Day Guide to Increase your EQ, Improve your Social Skills and Communication at Work, and Master Your Emotions* is about improving your social skills and becoming more socially competent.

This chapter of *The Ultimate 21-Day Guide to Increase your EQ, Improve your Social Skills and Communication at Work, and Master Your Emotions* will have you use the skills from the first four days' chapters in order to take an active stance that will allow you to initiate change in your environment. Learning to take this sort of action will be useful in helping you to become a more emotionally intelligent and socially adept individual. These skills can become crucial when working in the types of dynamic, variable, and fast-paced environments that are so common in today's work-centric society. As such, you will need to pay particularly close attention to the skills you learned in the first four days of this book's 21-day journey, as well as those from the chapters centered on the concepts of self-confidence, optimism, and self-control. When attempting to become a more emotionally flexible and innovative person, it is important to keep in mind that, while it can be very easy to overlook adaptability and innovativeness as valuable skills to be sought after, as they are extremely vital aspects of becoming emotionally intelligent and socially adept. Of course, you are allowed to circle back to previous chapters as needed, if you feel that it might be necessary or that you could be a little bit rusty on the topics they covered and their daily goals.

This chapter's assignment, of course, will be to actively take steps to make changes to and in your environment and life. In order to do this, you will need to follow the four-step guide set in the first four chapters, and use it to understand your current situation, formulate a plan for how you should act, and finally take action. The first step, of course, will be awareness. You will need to form a competent understanding of the five levels of emotional and social awareness and apply them to your current situation. Next, you will need to gain a thorough understanding of the information you have discerned. This should also be done while taking into account the information about your surroundings, with the ultimate goal of taking action to improve the situation.

Lastly, you will need to use the skills of emotional assessment and gauging needs from the lesson on day two to make a plan of action and follow it. This assignment will mirror the one from the fourth day's chapter. You should be actively choosing to remove yourself from uncomfortable situations or try to be putting yourself on ones that help your emotional states, when you decide on a certain solution or action to take in response to your emotional assessments and the conclusions that come from them. The goal for this assignment is to simply practice being active about improving your emotional states and promoting positivity for the sake of yourself and the people around you.

With all of that said, you should have all of the tools necessary to complete today's assignment and take another step on the path to self-improvement and mastering your emotions. Using the skills you learned previously, as with all assignments, will help you to ensure your success in this and all of the future chapters. Keeping this in mind, today's lesson should also be helpful, once it has been completed, for the assignments to come from the remaining days in this 21-day guide to improving your social skills and increasing your level of emotional intelligence.

Day 19:
How To Find Your Source Of Motivation And Inspiration

During yesterday's chapter in *The Ultimate 21-Day Guide to Increase your EQ, Improve your Social Skills and Communication at Work, and Master Your Emotions*, the topic of initiating change in your environment was discussed. It covered how to do so using the skills of adaptability and innovativeness, as well as the four skills learned during the book's first section, which included awareness, assessment, planning, and acting, in order to learn to make effective, meaningful, and unique changes in your environment. This is a valuable skill, as it will allow you to begin to think "outside of the box" and find effective solutions to unfamiliar or unexpected problems as they arise. It can also help you to be noticed and recognized for your achievements and accomplishments in a professional setting.

However, today's chapter will be covering the topic of finding a source of motivation or inspiration. This chapter will aim to help you Realize and maintain effective means of motivation, in both a micro and macro sense, as well as learning the difference between internal and external motivations and their sources. These concepts can be somewhat difficult to understand, and even more difficult to achieve, in many cases, but the best way to explain a person's source of motivation would be that it is the reason or reasons one has for acting or behaving in a particular way, or a person's general desire or willingness to do something. Of course, this is a fairly straightforward concept. The real trick is not in finding motivation, but in finding a source of motivation that is strong enough, and the "right" source for you. There is a saying that people will do anything for the right price, and to a certain extent, it is an accurate expression. Everyone has at least one thing that can be used as a reliable source of motivation to help them accomplish a goal or goals. In this case, the concepts of motivation, inspiration, and drive will be used in the context of emotional intelligence and the knowledge and mastery of emotional awareness, assessment, understanding, and management. This is an extremely important part of mastering your emotions and raising your emotional intelligence and your emotional quotient, as a positive attitude and trust in the idea of optimism can be extremely helpful, and even vital, on one's journey to mastering their emotions, raising their emotional intelligence and emotional quotient, and ultimately beginning to live the most emotionally satisfying and fulfilling life possible.

A very common misconception about the idea of motivation is that it comes as a result of consuming some fort of motivationally inspired media. While this is entirely possible, it is much more like and much more common to find a source of motivation only after picking up new behavior patterns, rather than before. Motivation is typically the result of taking action, not the result of it. This is why it is important to get started and to push yourself to take action, as this will help to build momentum. This is also why people say that things are hardest at the start. Once you have started, however, you will begin to require less and less in the way of active motivation. After you have started and made a little bit of progress, it becomes much more natural to continue with your task or tasks and accomplish your goals. As such, the first thing to keep in mind is that at first, you may not want to take action or may find it somewhat difficult to find the energy or motivation to keep going. This is why you should enforce the behaviors that you are attempting to pick up, if at all possible. It will become much easier to continue these behaviors once they have become habits. You should try to schedule times, for example, to exercise or study, and hold yourself to those scheduled times as much as possible. Turning these sorts of decisions into rituals and habits removes the need for active decisions to occur. This is the secret to staying driven and maintaining functionality. The more you deliberate, the more you hesitate, which can lead quickly to losing focus and giving up.

Another method for maintaining a sense of drive and staying motivated is to use what is referred to as the "Goldilocks Rule." This is a relatively straightforward concept. The story of Goldilocks and the Three Bears is about a young girl who wanders into the home of three bears looking for a meal. The first one is too hot, and the second too cold. The third one, however, is "just right." This can be applied to everyday life in order to gauge and alter levels of challenge and keep yourself motivated to continue moving forward. If, for example, you are playing a game with someone or doing some competitive activity with them. If they are too easy and you end up winning consistently every time, the challenge is too easy and will fail to stimulate you properly. As such, it will eventually stop being fun and you will grow restless. You might then give up and seek stimulation elsewhere, in a more challenging activity.

On the other hand, if it becomes too difficult, you might begin to perceive the task of success as impossible or unattainable. This can also be a problem, as it becomes very easy under these circumstances to simply give up, or lose interest in chasing a goal that seems impossible to reach. If you compare experiences similar to those described above to a situation wherein you may have competed against someone who was closer to your own skill level, the problem becomes obvious. When competing with someone who is "just right," you are usually able to win or succeed, but only if you really try and seek to improve. This is ideal, as your successes and failures will fluctuate, and it becomes much easier to maintain interest and motivation. Both or all parties will typically improve at similar rates, and you can maintain interest much longer. Hence the name, "The Goldilocks Rule." Human beings are much more likely to stay driven when their challenges and goals are at a level that is just right for them. As such, your task for today will be to attempt to find appropriate sources of motivation and set small, short-term goals that are stimulating and challenging, but also attainable. Ones that are "just right."

Inevitably, you will eventually begin to lose motivation. This can be temporary, provided you know and understand the steps necessary to avoid it impacting your sense of drive. One method is to consider that every thought you have is a suggestion, not an order. If you begin to feel tired, you are presented with a choice. You might also begin to think that if you hold off on rest for a little bit in order to accomplish a task, you will be able to accomplish your goal and experience the satisfaction that comes with. You will also experience the long-term benefits of this decision and can weigh the options in your mind. It is important to base your decisions on the paths that you think will be the most beneficial and healthy for you. Overall, despite whether or not they may seem more difficult in the immediate sense, it is also important to realize that discomfort is temporary, but the benefits you can experience as a result of hard work will last much longer, and possibly indefinitely. This sort of perspective can be extremely vital in staying driven and balancing responsibilities effectively. It is also important to remember that you should always be striving to improve and better yourself. Complacency is the killer of efficiency.

With all of that said, you should have all of the tools necessary to complete today's assignment and take another step on the path to self-improvement and mastering your emotions. Using the skills you learned previously, as with all assignments, will help you to ensure your success in this and all of the future chapters. Keeping this in mind, today's lesson should also be helpful, once it has been completed, for the assignments to come from the remaining days in this 21-day guide to improving your social skills and increasing your level of emotional intelligence.

Day 20:
Don't Stop Improving Yourself

During yesterday's chapter in *The Ultimate 21-Day Guide to Increase your EQ, Improve your Social Skills and Communication at Work, and Master Your Emotions*, the topic of motivation was talked about, including how to find, and maintain a sense of drive and what to do when you happen to lose your source of motivation. This is a valuable skill, as it will allow you to begin to think "outside of the box" and find effective solutions to unfamiliar or unexpected problems as they arise. It can also help you to be noticed and recognized for your achievements and accomplishments in a professional setting.

However, today's chapter will be covering the topic of striving for excellence, and why it is important to be aiming for improvement and self-betterment constantly. This chapter will aim to help you understand the meaning of the word excellence and what it means to "always be better." It will also go over the differences between excellence and perfection, and how to strive for excellence, as described above, without sacrificing innovation, as well as why this can be a difficult task. These concepts can be somewhat difficult to understand, and sometimes even more difficult to achieve but after reading today's chapter, you should possess all of the necessary information to understand and accomplish all of the tasks and goals set for the day.

Striving for excellence is an important part of professionalism at work, and of improving as a person in your daily life. It is all about trying to put meaningful work and emphasize quality in everything that you do, and this sort of attitude is what separates the good from the great when it comes to people and the things that they choose to spend their time on and with. In order to actually take the initiative and strive for excellence, it is necessary to take steps outside of your comfort zone, actively and regularly. You should always be attempting to put yourself in new or even uncomfortable situations and learning to adapt to those situations. As such, this is a goal for which you will need to utilize all of the tools you have gained over the last 19 days of reading this book. It is important to consider, however, that even if you are constantly striving to improve and better yourself in everything you do, you can never reach perfection. This may sound obvious, as no single person can ever hope to achieve perfection, but this is actually a very significant thing to keep in mind. This "Paradox of Perfection" is the exact reason why many individuals, along with the hard work involved, actually choose to opt out of this and other virtues of similar nature. No matter how hard you work to improve, you can never reach that 100% finish-line of absolute perfection. This does not mean, however, that it is pointless, or even that you should simply abstain from making an effort to improve altogether. It may even be arguable that the opposite is true. The absence of a concrete standard for optimal skill or form in any practice might be a reason to strive for excellence all on its own. The absence of such a goal means that there is no concrete, fixed line to signify the limit for our capacity for improvement. If we really wanted to, any one of us could become the best in the world in any given sport or practice, and there would still be competition simply because we will never lose our capacity for improvement. We can, and should, always be trying to become better than we were yesterday. "There is always someone better," after all.

It can be difficult to balance this skill with the skills from the last few chapters. Innovation might prove to be a particularly tricky skill to maintain while striving for excellence. People often say that laziness is the father of innovation and that if you want to innovate, you should strive not to achieve excellence, but to be different. There is also a quote from Bill Gates, "I choose a lazy person to do a hard job because that person will find an easy way to do it." This can make it seem very difficult or even impossible to balance these skills of innovation and excellence, but that is not always necessarily true. While it can be somewhat difficult, it is entirely possible to balance these skills with each other. You should always be attempting to change things to make them easier for yourself and others, and possess a certain amount of "laziness," but only so much that you can still push yourself in order to improve and strive for excellence in everything that you do.

Additionally, you should begin to focus on being, rather than having. This means that you should try to avoid using material gains as a source of motivation. Instead, you should be focused on experiences and your environment as motivators. You should attempt to define yourself based on who you are, rather than what you have. This will help you to form positive methods of motivating yourself and allow you to immerse yourself in your goals, and ultimately helping you to improve in everything you do, and accomplish the goals you set out to complete. It can also be helpful during the next and last assignment of *The Ultimate 21-Day Guide to Increase your EQ, Improve your Social Skills and Communication at Work, and Master Your Emotions*, which will focus on acceptance and learning to be okay with events as they are, especially if they can't be helped or changed. These skills can be extremely helpful, and even vital, on one's journey to mastering their emotions, raising their emotional intelligence and emotional quotient, and ultimately beginning to live the most emotionally satisfying and fulfilling life possible.

With all of that said, you should have all of the tools necessary to complete today's assignment and take another step on the path to self-improvement and mastering your emotions. Using the skills you learned previously, as with all assignments, will help you to ensure your success in this and all of the future chapters. Keeping this in mind, today's lesson should also be helpful, once it has been completed, for the assignments to come from the remaining days in this 21-day guide to improving your social skills and increasing your level of emotional intelligence.

Day 21:
Learning To Accept Situations That Are Out Of Your Control

During yesterday's chapter of *The Ultimate 21-Day Guide to Increase your EQ, Improve your Social Skills and Communication at Work, and Master Your Emotions*, the topic of excellence was talked about, including the meaning of the word excellence and what it means to "always be better." It also covered the differences between excellence and perfection, and how to strive for excellence without sacrificing innovation, as well as why that can sometimes be a difficult task. This is a valuable skill, as it will allow you to understand why it can be important, to strive for excellence in everything you do and how the simple act of trying to improve can be helpful in finding and maintaining motivation for your achievements and accomplishments in a professional setting as well as in your personal life.

However, today's chapter will be covering the topic of acceptance, and why it can be important to learn to accept situations that are out of your control, for the sake of your own mental and emotional health. The concepts of striving for excellence and acceptance can be somewhat contradictory. As such, this chapter will also go over the differences between these virtues, and why they are both important parts of emotional wellness, as well as how to balance them. True acceptance of one's situation can also be somewhat difficult to achieve, but after reading today's chapter, you should possess all of the necessary information to understand and accomplish all of the tasks and goals set for the day.

The actual definition of the word acceptance is the act of agreement with or belief in an idea, opinion, or explanation, or a willingness to tolerate a difficult or unpleasant situation. This means, in short, that acceptance is the ability to maintain contentedness with your current situation and situations that may be out of your control, especially difficult or unpleasant ones. This may seem to contradict the subject of the previous chapter, which was about striving for excellence in your professional and personal endeavors. Striving for excellence can be important, of course, but it can also be important to know when it is important to adapt and accept your current situation as it is, especially if it may be uncomfortable for you.

Mastering acceptance will take more than a single day, as it can be a lifelong goal to work toward. As was mentioned in the last chapter of this book, nobody can be perfect and being able to accept any and all situations that you may find yourself in, no matter how uncomfortable, is a very difficult, and possibly impossible task to accomplish. It is very important, however, to continue to be accepting, especially if the situation cannot be helped. This is actually part of the beauty of organic life. Nothing is constant, and the world around you is subject to change in ways that can have large or smaller effects on you and those around you. As such, it is very important to try to avoid wishing that something could be or could have been different, as you cannot change the past or present, only the future. This is the primary difference in situations that call for acceptance and striving for excellence. You should accept things that occurred in the past, and ones that are happening now, as they are impossible to change. Striving for excellence can only be applied in the present in order to improve conditions in the future, never the past. This will be the assignment for today, as well. You should be looking out for situations throughout the day, both positive and negative. While doing this, you will need to pay specific attention to the tenses of these situations, and whether it is more appropriate to apply the skills of acceptance or to strive for excellence, and act accordingly. This will be the last step to take on the road to mastering your emotional intelligence and raising your emotional quotient. It will give you all of the tools necessary in order to do so, and in turn, make you a much more emotionally healthy and well-rounded individual.

With all of that said, you should have all of the tools necessary to complete today's assignment and take another step on the path to self-improvement and mastering your emotions. Using the skills you learned previously, as with all assignments, will help you to ensure your success in this and all of the future chapters. Keeping this in mind, today's lesson should also be helpful, once it has been completed, for the assignments to come from the remaining days in this 21-day guide to improving your social skills and increasing your level of emotional intelligence.

Conclusion

Congratulations! You have officially completed all 21 days of *Ultimate 21-Day Guide to Increase your EQ, Improve your Social Skills and Communication at Work, and Master Your Emotions*. If you enjoyed this book, I'd really appreciate if you could take a few seconds to leave a short review on Amazon. Thank you, it means a lot to me!

You should now have all of the tools necessary to ensure your success in all of your future endeavors, now and in the future. This book was designed to help you to find the tools necessary in order to master your social skills and communication at work, as well as your emotions, which will in turn increase what is known as your Emotional Quotient and make you a much more emotionally healthy and well-rounded person.

The *Ultimate 21-Day Guide to Increase your EQ, Improve your Social Skills and Communication at Work, and Master Your Emotions* is, as it says on the cover, designed as a guide to help you improve your emotional intelligence and social skills, which covered 21 separate and extremely valuable lessons on this subject over the course of the aforementioned 21 days. As such, each lesson covered in its own day, so as to give you time to learn and master these skills. Over the course of this 21-day journey on the path to self-improvement and emotional wellness covered a number of complicated and difficult topics. The first four chapters discussed the topics necessary to give you the tools to help you in handling all of the topics to be handled over the following 17 days' chapters, as well as the assignments and goals involved. The next section, involving the fifth, sixth, seventh, and eighth days' chapters, was focused more on intrapersonal skills to help you understand yourself better, along with your emotional needs and how to control your own emotional states. The third section was centered around more social skills, to help you form bonds in professional and personal settings and improve your social skills to help you work well with others and even take on leadership roles effectively. The last chapter transitioned from those skills over to virtues that will help you achieve your goals and become a more emotionally healthy person in the general sense. These skills were important to finish off with, as they are lifelong goals that should always be aimed for, and are arguably the most important aspects to actually being emotionally healthy as a person. Obviously, you can't be expected to master your emotions in just 21 days completely. Many, and possibly even all of the tasks and goals that were set over the course of the 21 days of this book's journey are ones that require multiple days, or even extended periods of time in order to complete. Especially complicated lessons, such as striving for excellence, for example, require daily attention, and may never even cease to be a goal to be reaching for constantly.

With all of that said and out of the way, I would like to thank you again for taking the initiative of purchasing this book and offer congratulations for choosing to better yourself in such a way. As has been stated previously, you are also allowed to circle back and revisit old chapters as you see fit, and I would urge you to do so. It can be very easy to forget, in difficult or high-pressure situations, some important lessons, and you may find yourself needing a small reminder of why these skills can be important or how to maintain them. In this sort of event, this book can prove to be a valuable resource, and should definitely be utilized in order to assist you in living the most emotionally satisfying and fulfilling life that you are capable of living.

Other Books by Judith Yandell

EMPATH

SURVIVAL AND HEALING GUIDE FOR
EMPATHS AND HIGHLY SENSITIVE PEOPLE
TO SHIELD YOURSELF FROM NEGATIVE ENERGIES,
MANAGE YOUR EMPATHY AND DEVELOP YOUR GIFT

JUDITH YANDELL

We all feel some kind of empathy towards others. But if you have no control over your empathy and always have the obsession of fixing other people, then you know how painfully frustrating being an empath is.

Empaths are usually overwhelmed by other people's emotions, they feel what others feel and are able to profoundly understand their mind. As a result, empaths care for everyone else but themselves. They become "magnets" for negative people that want to take advantage of the empaths' ability to understand opinions and emotions of others.

However, I want you to know that being an empath doesn't have to be so negative. You may have not yet realized it, but you have a powerful and beautiful gift. If you learn how to embrace it and channel your empathy, you can use it for spreading kindness, love and positive energy to the world.

In this book you'll learn:
- 6 Powerful Methods You Can Use to Control Your Gift (Hint: They Don't Include "Avoid Social Situations" and "Lock Yourself Up in You House")
- The Single Most Effective Thing You Can Do to Shield Yourself From Energy Vampires
- 11 Most Common Personality Traits of Empaths
- Powerful Techniques to Develop Your Skills and Channel Your Empathy to Spread Positive Energy
- How To Use a Specific Kind of Negative Thinking to Actually Overcome Your Social Anxiety
- 20 Statements to Help You Determine if You Really Are an Empath
- Is an Energy Vampire Preying on You? Here's How to Find Out
- How to Find Out if Your Child Is an Empath and What You Can Do to Support
- A Positive Affirmations Routine That Can Help You Accept Yourself as an Empath and Strengthen Your Abilities
- How Detoxifying a Certain Area of Your Brain Can Help You Embrace Your Empathic Abilities and Improve Your Sense of Intuition

- Why in Certain Cases Accepting Negativity Can Actually Help You Feel Better.

Even if right now you feel you have no control over your abilities, I want you to know that you can learn how to manage your empathy and develop your gift in the right way.

**"Empath" by Judith Yandell
is available at Amazon.**

JUDITH YANDELL

BUDDHISM
FOR BEGINNERS

PLAIN AND SIMPLE GUIDE TO BUDDHIST PHILOSOPHY
INCLUDING ZEN TEACHINGS, TIBETAN BUDDHISM
AND MINDFULNESS MEDITATION

Do You Want To Free Yourself From Stress And Anxiety? Would you like to bring peace and joy in your life?

Many people hear the word "Buddhism" and they think it is a religion. However, a person of any religion can bring Buddhist principles into their life without giving up their religious beliefs.

Buddhism is a simple and practical philosophy, practiced by more than 300 million people worldwide, that can make your life better and help you find inner peace and happiness.

Buddhism is a way of living your life following a path of spiritual development that leads you to the truth of reality.

"We are shaped by our thoughts; we become what we think. When the mind is pure, joy follows like a shadow that never leaves." - Buddha

Nowadays, Buddhism is becoming increasingly popular, thanks to the positive benefits it can bring to those who choose to practice it.

By following the principles of Buddhism and by practicing mindfulness meditation you can reduce anxiety and stress and bring clarity and joy into your mind.

If you want to learn how to apply the Buddhist philosophy in your everyday life, then this book is for you.

You'll learn the principles of this philosophy along with the history of Buddha and his teachings that will help you successfully bring Buddhism into your everyday life.

This book will give you the answers you're seeking in a format that is both simple and easy to understand, without obscure words or convoluted sentences.

Inside Buddhism for Beginners, discover:

- How you can bring peace and joy in your life following the simple principles of Buddhism
- A simple but effective meditation technique for beginners to help you relieve stress and feel calmer, even if you've never meditated before

- The core Buddhist principles and teachings explained in plain english, without complex or obscure words
- The History of Buddhism, from its origins to the present day
- Why knowing and freeing your mind can help you bring peace and joy in your everyday life (with practical tips to help you start)
- A complete historical timeline of notable buddhist events to help you understand the development of this philosophy
- The principles you should pursue if you want to follow the path of Buddha
- An effective way to understand and practice Buddhism without feeling overwhelmed
- The truth about Karma and how it can actually help you change your life (many people don't know this)
- Practical tips to bring Buddhism into your everyday life and brighten your future.
- And much, much more.

Now it's up to you. Even if right now you have no clue of Buddha's teachings, let joy and peace become part of your life and free you from stress and anxiety, you won't regret it!

"Buddhism for Beginners" by Judith Yandell is available at Amazon.